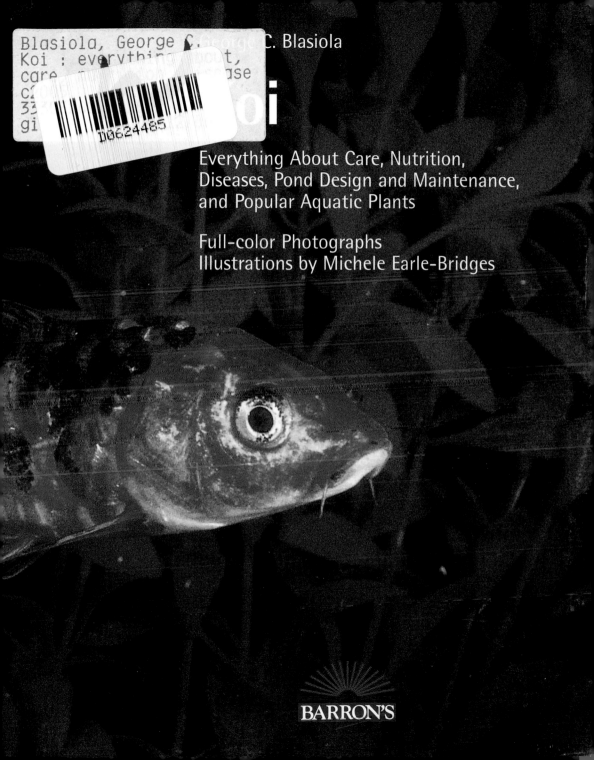

George C. Blasiola

# Koi

Everything About Care, Nutrition,
Diseases, Pond Design and Maintenance,
and Popular Aquatic Plants

Full-color Photographs
Illustrations by Michele Earle-Bridges

**BARRON'S**

# CONTENTS

# MORPHOLOGY AND VARIETIES OF KOI

*The origin of koi, the most popular of all pondfish worldwide, dates back many centuries. The colorful koi varieties that we see in ponds today are descendents of the drab-colored wild carp that lived in streams in Asia and Europe.*

Koi, or *nishikigoi* (Japanese for "colored koi"), are the most popular freshwater fish among pond owners. Their beauty, grace, and brilliant colors have made them the world's favorite ornamental fish. Because they combine ease of care, longevity, adaptation to most pond environments, and often striking color variations, they are eagerly sought by owners throughout the world. Over the past several decades, new varieties (types) have become available for stocking ponds. So brilliant are their colors that some people have referred to them as "living jewels."

Symbols of strength and masculinity in Japan, koi are known there as the "warrior's fish." The Japanese regard them as symbols of good luck and prosperity. Each year in the month of May, beautiful *koinobori* (streamers) in the shape of koi are flown from poles in celebration of the Boy's Day Festival. The streamers symbolize the Japanese parents' hope that

*Koi, also known as* **nishikigoi**, *are the most popular fish in the world for keeping in ponds.*

their sons will demonstrate courage and strength, like that of the *nishikigoi*.

Due to the many color variations and patterns, koi are sometimes thought to be different species, yet they are all *Cyprinus carpio*. There are some apparent exceptions, such as the novel butterfly koi, but these are hybrids created by mating closely related carp.

## Morphological Features

The colorful koi, *Cyprinus carpio*, are classified as bony fish in the *Cyprinidae*. This family is represented by numerous related fish, including goldfish and minnows. There are various morphological features that characterize these beautiful pondfish.

Ornamental koi are domesticated carp that have been selectively bred for their colors and patterns. They are freshwater, bottom-dwelling fish, inhabiting temperate climates but capable of living in a wide range of conditions.

Wild carp, the ancestors of the koi, are found in lakes and streams worldwide. They feed on plants, worms, insects, etc. Carp can reach a length of over 3 feet (91 cm) and weight in excess of 25 pounds (11.3 kg).

Koi are long-lived fish, with individuals known to have survived well over 40 years. However, reports of Japanese koi living to an age of more than 200 years are probably more myth than fact.

# General External Features

**Medial fins:** These are all single. The large dorsal (top) fin, which extends backward, is lowered during rapid swimming and helps maintain the fish upright in the water. The forked caudal (tail) fin is used to propel the fish forward. On the koi's ventral (bottom) surface a single anal fin helps to stabilize the fish during swimming.

**Lateral fins:** These fins are paired. The pelvic fins, located in front of the anal fin, enable the fish to move up and down in the water. And just behind the gill covers are the pectoral fins, which are used in braking and making turns.

**Mouth:** Koi are essentially bottom feeders although they are capable of feeding on materials at any water level. Their mouth can be protruded and it is located at the end of the snout, slightly below the midline.

**Barbels:** These are richly endowed with sensory receptors that enable koi to detect food particles in sand or mud without the need for visual information. Just above the barbels, almost between the eyes, are a pair of nostrils that are used to detect odors.

**Ears:** Koi possess organs of hearing similar to other vertebrates, but there are no external "ears." The internal ear detects sound in association with the swim bladder.

**Nostrils:** A pair of nostrils are present, located between the eyes and mouth. The olfactory organs called nares are present at the basal portion and used to detect dissolved chemical compounds in the water.

**Lateral lines:** Close examination of the sides of the koi will reveal a series of small pores that run approximately midline from head to the tail. These are termed the *lateral lines*. Their purpose is to detect low-frequency vibrations in the water, such as might be generated by a large predator.

**Eyes:** These are located behind the nostrils. Koi lack true eyelids, the covering of the eye being simply a layer of transparent *epithelium* (skin). The lens is spherical and rigid, providing focus by moving forward or back within the eye.

**Gills:** Respiratory structures situated behind the eyes in *branchial chambers*, each set of gills is covered by a flap of skin and bone called an *operculum*, which moves water across the feathery gills. The gills themselves contain specialized tissues with rich capillary networks designed for gas exchange. Dissolved oxygen is taken in from the water and carbon dioxide and ammonia are released.

**Scales:** The body is typically covered with a large number of small scales, though there are breeds that have a lesser number of large scales, and others in which the scales are absent. Scales are not present on the head. Some varieties, most notably the *doitsu* koi (German-scaled), only have scales present along the lateral line.

The scales, when present, overlap and project out of the dermal layer (skin) at an angle. They are covered with a layer of mucus, which reduces friction as the fish swims.

**Colors:** The colors of koi are a function of the type and distribution of pigments within the fish's skin. Within certain of the dermal cells are tiny sacs of pigment called *chromatophores*. These pigment sacs can contain several types of pigments, including *melanin* (black) and the *carotenoids* that give the beautiful and well-known red and orange colors. In addition to these pigments, koi also have cells called *iridocytes*, which contain guanine crystals. It is these crystals that give the silver or gold metallic appearance to the koi's skin.

# Basic Koi Classification

The Japanese classify koi varieties according to various features, including color, patterns, and scale type and arrangement. There is an economic and esthetic hierarchy of form, color, and pattern that determines the desirability and value of particular koi.

Japanese terminology ranges from down-to-earth description to poetic analogy to political reference. The actual words used to discuss these animals are typically untranslated Japanese, and the meaning of the names is frequently lost to the Western fancier.

# Koi Terminology Explained

All the major varieties have their specific names, and subvarieties within the variety will have their own names as well. For example, a major variety, the *kohaku*, has red and white markings, while another major variety, the *sanke*, has black and red patterns on a white background. Another subvariety is the *tansho kohaku*. This red and white fish with a large red mark on its head borrows its name from the red-crested crane.

Names can also refer to specific coloration patterns. An example of this is a *kohaku* with a

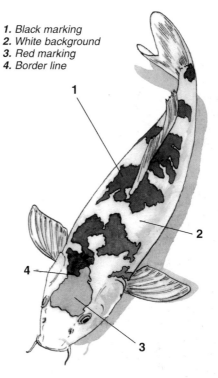

1. *Black marking*
2. *White background*
3. *Red marking*
4. *Border line*

*Body patterns are one of the characteristics used to classify koi. The tancho sanke has a white background, black patterns, and a red patch on its head.*

cluster of red spots. This particular type is referred to as a *gotenzakura*, which translates as "palace cherry blossoms."

## Coloration

As a general rule, koi will bear from one to three body colors. Various koi represented in the single-color koi group include

✔ orange *ogon* (orange)
✔ *ki-goi* (yellow)
✔ *shiro* (white)
✔ *muji* (flat)
✔ *ogon* (metallic)

*Asagi koi were developed approximately 150 years ago.*

*This leather type koi is classified as a doitsu shiro bekko.*

*Shusui are often quite striking fish with large doitsu scales and beautiful colors.*

*Hikarimoyo are koi with two colors, one of which is metallic.*

**Bekko** *koi have patterns that resemble a tortoise shell. Note the characteristic black patches* (**sumi**) *on this* aka bekko.

*Kin ki utsuri koi are classified within the hikari utsuri group: koi that are bicolored with distinctive metallic scales.*

*A beautiful* **shiro bekko** *koi.*

*The goshiki is a popular and prized fish.*

Ginrin bekko *with a striking tortoise shell* pattern.

Aigoromo *are produced by crossing an* asagi *with a* kohaku.

*A* stunning ginrin kohaku *with the characteristic metallic sheen on its scales.*

*This* inazuma kohaku *is named for the lightning-like pattern on its back.*

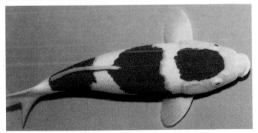

Kohaku *have red markings on a white background. This prize-winning* kohaku *koi is a superb example.*

*The* Showa sanke *group, also referred to as* Showa, *are koi with red and white markings on a black background.*

*A* yamabuki ogon.

*A* kin matsuba ogon.

Koi in the double-color group are described by names that can be one or two words. In binomial appellations the second word refers to the background color of the fish. The term "background" is given to the color that occupies the greatest area of skin. A common koi variety in this group, widely available and familiar to many pond owners, is the previously mentioned red and white *kohaku*. Other varieties in this two-color category include *shiro utsuri* (white and black), *shiro bekko* (black and white), and *ki utsuri* (yellow and black). The word *utsuri* means reflection; therefore, the koi variety *ki-utsuri* translates to "yellow koi with a reflection."

The third group consists of koi varieties with three body colors. These koi represent some of the most popular pond varieties. They include the *Showa sanke* (black background with white and red mottles) and *Taisho sanke* (white background with black and red mottles).

## Patterning

The Japanese also use terms to describe specific patterns of coloration. For example, there is a popular *kohaku* (red and white) with a pattern on its back that resembles lightning. It is called *inazuma hi* (red lightning). Another example is the previously mentioned *tancho kohaku*, with red markings on the top of its head.

## Scalation

The scale pattern (or absence of scales) is an additional characteristic used in describing koi. In some varieties it is the dominant esthetic consideration. An example would be the *doitsu* (German-scaled), a hybrid of German and Japanese koi. This is a type with a reduced number of scales, first bred in Germany during the early 1900s. Some of these fish were eventually introduced into Japan, where they were crossed with Japanese koi. *Doitsu* have large, sparse scales. Occasionally, the scales are entirely lacking, and the fish are then referred to as "leather koi."

*Doitsu* are subdivided into types and include *kani goi*, which are scaleless; *kagami goi*, which have large scales on the dorsal and ventral portions of the body; and *ara doitsu*, which have large scales with an irregular arrangement all over the body.

# Varieties and Types

While there are a limited number of major koi varieties, there are numerous subvarieties or *types*. To the Japanese, many of these types are considered to be of "low quality" if they lack desirable characteristics of the varietal group. It is important not to consider the groupings synonymous with "pedigrees," as this is not always the case with koi. It is the actual physical characteristics of a given koi that determine its classification, not its pedigree line.

# The Classification System

The Japanese classification system is a complicated one. It is basically comprised of 13 major varieties, which are used consistently for judging koi during competitions.

The following varieties are recognized, although others will undoubtedly be added in the future as new strains are developed:

✔ *Asagi* and *Shusui*
✔ *Bekko*
✔ *Hikarimoyo mono*
✔ *Hikari utsuri mono*
✔ *Kawari mono*
✔ *Kinginrin*

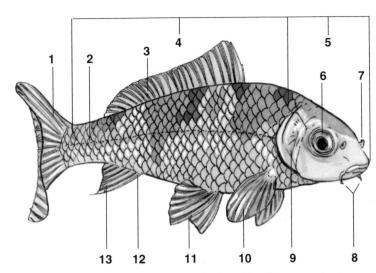

1. Caudal fin
2. Lateral line
3. Dorsal fin
4. Body
5. Head
6. Eye
7. Nostril
8. Barbels
9. Operculum
10. Pectoral fins
11. Pelvic fins
12. Anal pore
13. Anal fin

*The external morphological features of a koi,* Cyprinus carpio *(see pages 6–7).*

✔ Kohaku
✔ Koromo
✔ Ogon
✔ Showa sanke
✔ Taisho sanke
✔ Utsuri mono
✔ Tancho

## 1. Asagi and Shusui

These two koi varieties are traditionally combined in one category during Japanese koi competitions.

*Asagi* ("light blue") are predominantly blue or gray on their backs, while the underside is generally red or orange. The scales tend to be light in color and can be patterned in either the normal or *doitsu* types.

There are various types of *asagi*, of which the most important are:
✔ *Asagi sanke*, which have an *asagi* pattern with red on the abdomen and head region and a white underside.

✔ *Konjo asagi*, which possess a coloration ranging from dark gray to black. This type is rather out of favor among Japanese fanciers these days.
✔ *Mizu asagi*, which are highly prized, light blue fish.
✔ *Taki asagi*, which are blue on the back and red on the abdominal area, with an intersecting band of white.

*Shusui* ("autumn water") resemble *asagi koi,* but they occur only as *doitsu.*

Some representative types include
✔ *Hi shusui*, which have a red color (*hi*) on the back. The large *doitsu* scales on the back are blue and extend from the head to the tail.
✔ *Ki shusui*, which have the characteristic *shusui* body, but with yellow and dark blue on the back.
✔ *Hana shusui*, which have red markings on both sides of the body and abdomen, extending to the tail.
✔ *Pearl shusui*, having *doitsu* scales with a glittering pearly appearance.

*A doitsu showa.*

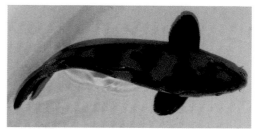

Hi utsuri *have red markings on a black background.*

*The* Taisho sanke *or tricolor has black and red accent coloration on a white body background.*

*The* tancho Showa *has the markings of a* Showa sanke *but without the* tancho *head marking.*

Kuchibeni Taisho sanke *have red on the snout and lips.*

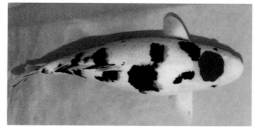

*A* tancho sanke *with a strong* tancho *mark on the head.*

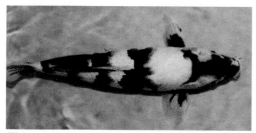

Shiro utsuri *display white markings on a black background.*

*This is an excellent example of a* tancho kohaku.

## 2. Bekko

This variety was developed during the *Bunka* (1804–1917) and *Bunsei* (1818–1929) eras. It has patterns that resemble those of a tortoise shell. The primary color can be red, orange, yellow, or white, highlighted by black patterns on the upper body.

Variations within this category include

✔ *Aka bekko*, which have *sumi* on a basic red background.

✔ *Ki bekko*, which have *sumi* on a yellow background.

✔ *Shiro bekko*, which are primarily white with black sumi accents and no red markings. Black stripes can be present on the pectoral fins.

✔ *Doitsu bekko*, which can have either scaleless "leather" bodies or mirror scales.

## 3. Hikarimoyo Mono

The Japanese word *moyo* translates as "pattern," while *hikari* means "metallic." Fish in this group will have two colors—one metallic, the other flat. The metallic color should be bright, meaning white fish should have a deep platinum color, black fish a jet black, and red fish the appearance of copper. The head region should be free of any spots, which are considered to be defects. For example, a platinum fish should not have black marks (*sumi*) on the head.

Several representative types within the grouping are

✔ *Hariwake*, which have gold and silver patterns on the body and fins. The head region is usually of one color and free of marks.

✔ *Kinsui*, which have a metallic red coloration.

✔ *Yamabuki*, which have a yellow and platinum coloration.

✔ *Yamatonishiki*, a favorite of koi fanciers, which has a beautiful metallic appearance.

## 4. Hikari Utsuri Mono

The *hikari utsuri* group is comprised of bicolored fish with distinctive metallic scales. Other colors can be present, including black and red.

Types within this category include

✔ *Kin ki utsuri*, which have a beautiful metallic yellow color.

✔ *Kin Showa*, which have a metallic gold color, developed during the Showa era (1926–1989).

✔ *Gin Showa*, which have a silver or platinum color.

## 5. Kawari Mono

This is the "catch-all" term, as all koi that do not fit into other categories are placed within this group. Some of the types include

✔ *Karasu goi*, which have an overall black color ranging from light gray to deep black.

✔ *Ki goi*, with a yellow body and variable coloration on the fins. They can possess normal or *doitsu* scalation, and, if the latter, can be either leather or mirror-scale type.

✔ *Kumonryu*, a predominantly black type with an irregular white line on the back and sides. The pectoral fins can be either solid white or black and white. The name translates as "dragon with nine markings."

✔ *Goshiki*, one of the most prized koi, distinguished by a combination of five body colors. This type is predominantly black with accents of red, white, brown, and blue. Goshiki are produced by crossing an *asagi* with an *aka sanke*.

## 6. Kinginrin

This group is also metallic, but the metallic sheen tends to be brighter with numerous silver body markings. The distribution and appearance of the silver on the scales is variable. The scales are also referred to by different names, depending on their characteristics. For example, scales that have a high luster and strongly reflect the silver color are called *beta gin*.

Variations are abundant in this group. Several common ones are

✔ *Ginrin*, whose silver-colored scales appear on the white portion of the fish's body.
✔ *Kinginrin bekko*, a black fish with silver markings on the body scales.
✔ *Kinginrin kohaku*, on which the red and white body has a scattering of silver on the scales, giving an interesting glittering appearance.
✔ *Kinginrin sanke*, with silver scales on the red, black, and white body.

## 7. Kohaku

Good-quality *kohaku* should have brilliant red markings on a pure white body color and a red pattern on the head. Their scalation can be either normal or *doitsu*.

There are numerous types occurring within this category, including

✔ *Aka muji*, a predominantly red fish.
✔ *Shiro muji*, a predominantly white fish. Better-quality *shiro muji* are free of black spots or other dark pigmented markings.
✔ *Inazuma* has a lightning-like pattern present on the dorsal surface of the fish, usually extending down the entire back. Higher-quality fish have an unbroken pattern with a good red color present.
✔ *Kuchibeni*, which has red color present on the head region and on the lips. This type is not favored in Japan.
✔ *Omoyo*, which has a large, red wavy pattern on the back.

## 8. Koromo

This variety is less common than some of the others. It is characterized by red and white coloration, with an overlay of blue or silver over the background. *Koromo* translates as "robed," a description of the overall appearance of the color patterns.

Some types within this group are

✔ *Aigoromo*, a hybrid produced by crossing an *asagi* with a *kohaku*. The fish has a distinctive blue edging on the red background.
✔ *Budo sanke*, an uncommon type with a white background on which are found black and blue markings that give the appearance of bunches of grapes.
✔ *Koromo sanke*, which has blue markings on the red areas of the fish's body. It is produced by breeding a *Taisho sanke* with an *aigoromo*.

## 9. Ogon

A well-known and popular variety, the *ogon* has a uniform metallic-gold body color varying in hue from light to dark. Among the types within this group are

✔ *Doitsu ogon*, which can be either mirror scale or leather type.
✔ *Hi ogon*, which have a red body color. The body area is generally uniform, with streaks of off-white to yellow.
✔ *Kin matsuba*, a golden type with dark color present in the center of the scales, giving a reticulated appearance to the body. *Matsuba* translates as "pine needles."
✔ *Ogon*, which have a body coloration ranging from yellow to yellow-orange. Other *ogon* koi have a silvery color often referred to as platinum.

## 10. Showa Sanke

The *Showa sanke*, also referred to simply as *Showa*, is primarily black with red and white markings. It was developed by breeding a *kohaku* with a *ki utsuri*.

This variety can easily be confused with the *Taisho sanke*, described below. To differentiate them, bear in mind that the *Taisho sanke's* black coloration is present on the dorsal area, the pectoral fins are colorless, and black coloration is absent from the head region. The *Showa sanke's* black coloration, on the other hand, extends to the abdomen, while the pectoral fins and head are black.

Types within this group include

✔ *Boke Showa*, which are lighter in color, and which may have a bluish appearance. The black coloration is usually not well defined.

✔ *Doitsu Showa*, with mirror-type scales, or none at all.

✔ *Hi Showa*, in which red predominates on the dorsal portion and there is only a minor amount of white. The red color normally extends from the head region to the tail.

## 11. Taisho Sanke

The *Taisho sanke* is another popular koi variety. It is also referred to as a *sanshoku*, which translates as "tricolor." This variety was developed during the Taisho era (1912–1926). It is characterized by a white background with black and red accent coloration.

Several representative types within the *Taisho sanke* category include

✔ *Aka sanke*, which are mostly red.

✔ *Doitsu sanke*, which have a small number of large mirror scales or no scales at all.

✔ *Kuchibeni*, which have red on the snout and lips.

## 12. Utsuri Mono

This variety is distinguished by a black background and white, red, or yellow markings. The black pectoral fins tend to be triangular in shape. It is older than the *sankes*, having been developed during the Meiji era (1867–1912).

Representative types include

✔ *Shiro utsuri*, with white body patterns.

✔ *Hi utsuri*, with red body patterns.

✔ *Ki utsuri*, with orange or yellow markings.

✔ *Doitsu utsuri*, with scalation as described above.

## 13. Tancho

The body is a uniform white color, and there is a distinctive red pattern on the top of the head. Quality is judged by the uniformity and purity of the white background and the shape and extent of the head marking. Some varieties within the group include

✔ *Tancho kohaku*, in which the only red area is on the head.

✔ *Tancho Showa*, which have the typical *Showa sanke* pattern (see above) with the distinctive *tancho* head mark.

✔ *Tancho sanke*, with white body coloration, black patterns, and the *red tancho* head patch.

# PLANNING AND INSTALLING A POND

*Planning and designing a pond offers various possibilities for the koi enthusiast; ponds can be constructed with a variety of materials*

## Designing a Koi Pond

A properly designed pond will provide a healthy aquatic environment. Consideration must be given to the pond type, material used for construction, and selection of equipment and type of filtration, among other factors. Standard guidelines should be followed when setting up a koi pond. Hasty design can result in high maintenance as well as costly modifications to the system.

## Pond Types and Materials

Koi ponds can be constructed from various materials, including plastic liners (PVC), synthetic rubber-based liners (EPDM), preformed fiberglass, reinforced plastic, and concrete.

*Various types of ponds can be designed, from formal concrete ponds to a simple informal plastic-lined pond. Careful planning is the key to pond design.*

### Plastic Liners

Plastic liners have been widely used for the construction of ponds in past years. Their versatility and economical cost have allowed many people to design and install a pond. A pond employing polyvinyl chloride (PVC) can often be installed over a weekend. Unlike the rigid design of preformed fiberglass, liners can be adapted to any shape. They are available in various sizes, colors, and thicknesses. A liner of 32 mil thickness can be expected to last up to 10 years.

In addition to PVC, another material has become popular in recent years for the construction of ponds. Known as EPDM (ethylene propylene diene monomer) this rubber-based liner material has quickly replaced the use of PVC due to many of the materials' improved characteristics. It has a much longer use life ranging between 20 and 25 years, is able to withstand UV exposure better, has the ability to resist cracking, is suitable for all weather use, and is highly flexible. Like PVC the material

TIP

## Liners

Use only liners approved for use with fish, as some types are unsafe. Industrial liners, including many of those sold at hardware stores and home improvement centers, are treated with algicides and other chemicals that could be harmful to fish and water plants.

easily conforms to designing any shape of pond desired. Should any tears occur, the tear can easily be repaired using adhesive designed for use with the liner material.

The liner material EPDM is available in 45 mil thickness and various sizes. The material can be purchased from various pond suppliers in pre-cut sizes ranging from 8 × 10 feet (2.4 × 3 m) up to 25 × 30 feet (7.6 × 9 m) or larger. Multiple sizes can be joined together to accommodate larger-sized ponds using the adhesive to join the panels. An optional underlay material is available for placement in the excavated pond prior to placement of the EPDM liner.

Although plastic liners have the disadvantage of tearing on occasion, they can be repaired using special PVC glue or EPDM adhesive and a patch of the liner material. Also, careful handling and limited use of maintenance equipment that could puncture the liner will minimize the problem.

## Rigid Fiberglass and Plastic Ponds

Fiberglass ponds, especially the preformed type, are very popular, due to their low cost and ease of installation. They are excellent for the neophyte.

Preformed fiberglass reinforced ponds are available in various sizes and shapes, including free-form and geometrics. They are weather-resistant and, depending on the material from which they are constructed, will generally withstand ice formation during the winter. Many suppliers will also predrill them for filtration piping and drains. Fiberglass ponds are an excellent way to get started with your first koi pond.

Preformed plastic ponds are generally too small to be considered for a koi pond. They are susceptible to deterioration when exposed to sunlight and tend to crack within a relatively short period of time.

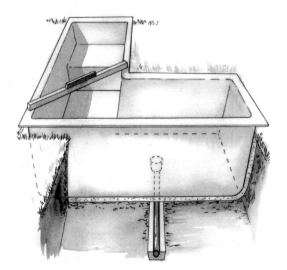

*Fiberglass pond manufacturers will predrill the shell for filtration piping and drains. It is important to make sure that the pond is perfectly level during installation.*

## Concrete Ponds

Concrete ponds can be custom-built to fit into any garden landscape. They are more costly to engineer and construct, but when properly designed, they will outlast many other materials.

# Pond Size

Koi ponds must be designed to accommodate the size and number of fish you have selected, taking into consideration the fact that they will grow. As a general recommendation, ponds should not be any smaller than 300 gallons (1135 L). While it is possible to keep a number of koi in smaller volumes of water, maintenance of water quality is more difficult in smaller ponds. The smaller the volume, the more quickly the pond will foul. Small ponds will also undergo more extreme fluctuations in temperature. Crowding of koi must be avoided to minimize the stress and uncleanliness that predispose koi to disease.

# Water Depth

A uniform pond depth must be avoided, as this poses problems in maintenance, water temperature fluctuation, and difficulty in protecting the fish from predators. Generally, the depth of the shallow zone should not exceed 20 inches (50.8 cm), sloping into water with a depth of about 36 inches (91 cm). Depths of 16 to 20 inches (40.6–50.8 cm) are sufficient in warm regions such as Florida, California, and Hawaii. In colder areas that are subject to freezing, water depths of 48 inches (122 cm) or more may be required.

Shallow areas should slope at a steep angle into deeper pond zones. A deep central area of

## TIP

### Deeper Zones

Deeper zones in the pond serve as refuge areas where the koi can retreat from predators, as well as providing cooler zones during the summer months. In colder regions, deep areas provide a place where koi can hibernate during the winter months, safe from the layer of ice.

the pond allows for the gradual movement of debris toward that region, where it is more easily removed. A sump with a grate connected to a drain can be installed in nonliner-type ponds; this will remove debris to a sewer.

The range of depths will serve a number of purposes. Shallow areas around the edges of the pond can be used for observation and for feeding the koi. The shallow zones can also be used for planting various types of aquatic plants that are intolerant of deeper water.

# Pond Location

Ideally, koi ponds should be located in areas providing partial shade at some time during the day. Ponds situated in full sunlight often develop algae blooms, although sunlight is only one factor encouraging such developments.

On the other hand, the pond should be located in an area free of overhanging tree branches and bushes. While some vegetation can be planted nearby to provide some shade, the vegetation should not extend over the pond. In addition, make sure that the pond is not situated close to trees that could cause problems in

*Concrete ponds are more costly to build but can be customized to just about any garden landscape. This pond was designed to withstand the cold winters in Cold Spring, New York.*

*Pre-formed fiberglass ponds are available in several shapes and sizes.*

### TIP

**Pre-formed Plastic Ponds**

Preformed plastic ponds are not recommended for use outdoors. They can, however, be used as emergency containers, or as temporary holding facilities and quarantine tanks.

the future. Developing tree roots will eventually crack nearby walkways and can cause damage to the pond structure. The decomposition of fallen leaves in ponds results in the development of acid conditions. The accumulation of organics in the bottom sediment promotes the development of anaerobic bacteria, which release toxic chemicals such as methane and hydrogen sulfide. Overhanging evergreens, such as spruce and pine, must be avoided—the falling needles leach toxic substances into the water.

In selecting a pond location you should also consider the accessibility of electrical connections.

## Landscaping

It is important to prevent the entry of runoff water into the pond. Heavy water runoff carries organic materials, soil, fertilizers, insecticides, and other materials. The perimeters of below-grade ponds should be raised to prevent drainage from adjacent lawns during watering of plants and rainstorms. This can be accomplished by the installation of edging around the pond, using rock, wood, or other materials. It is essential to incorporate drains around the pond perimeter and nearby walkways to channel water away from the pond.

*The edging of any pond can be made more attractive by using flagstones or other native rock materials.*

The most serious problem with water runoff is the potential accumulation of fertilizers and pesticides in the pond water.

## Filtration Requirements

Filtration is necessary to minimize maintenance and to preserve a healthy pond environment.

The use of recirculated water through water purification devices (filters) is the most common method of conditioning. The selection of a proper filtration system is an extremely important decision for the koi pond owner. This is an area where you should not attempt to economize, as the ultimate success of the pond rests on the quality of the filter equipment. (A detailed discussion of filtration begins on page 41.)

## Aeration

It is recommended that supplemental aeration be provided in ponds to maintain dissolved oxygen levels at acceptable concentrations. Large surface areas of ponds allow excellent gas exchange, but accessory agitation is always desirable.

Aeration accomplishes two important objectives:

✔ It maximizes the concentration of dissolved oxygen required by the fish and by the filter bacteria.

✔ It permits rapid dispersion of carbon dioxide and other gases from the water.

# CHECKLIST

## Avoiding Electrical Accidents

It is important to use caution when handling electrical equipment and wiring, which are particularly hazardous when used in connection with water. Always observe the following safeguards carefully:

**1** Before using any of the electrical equipment described in this book, check to be sure that it carries the UL symbol.

**2** Keep all lamps away from water or spray.

**3** Before using any equipment in water, check the label to make sure it is suitable for underwater use.

**4** Disconnect the main electrical plug before you begin any work in a pond or touch any equipment.

**5** Be sure that the electric current you use passes through a central fuse box or circuit-breaker system. Such a system should be installed only by a licensed electrician.

**6** The installation of ground fault circuit interrupter (GFCI) on outside devices, especially those near the pond, is an important means of preventing accidental electrocution, both of yourself and of your koi.

**Note:** It is important to employ aeration devices when using well water. Water from this source is often low in oxygen, sometimes containing less than 1 part per million. Well water should be aerated to add oxygen and drive off any excess carbon dioxide.

Aeration of new water can be accomplished through fountains, waterfalls, or other methods.

# TIP

## Electrical Fences

Never run electrical fences on house current; a transformer must be used. Also, make sure you check local ordinances regarding the installation of such devices in your yard.

It is important that the water be kept in motion. Stagnant conditions result in serious water-quality deterioration.

Care must be given to avoiding excessive agitation, however, since under certain conditions this can induce supersaturation of nitrogen.

## Pond Skimmers

Ponds should incorporate some method of skimming the water to remove film, floating algae, and other materials that often collect on the pond surface. A pond skimmer will make maintenance easier by consolidating leaves and other floating debris in a collecting basket that can easily be cleaned. Skimmers are connected to the pump that pulls water into the filtration system.

Skimmers are generally incorporated into the design of concrete pools, and it is possible to incorporate them into other types of pools as well.

## Water Evaporation

Because water is continually lost from ponds by evaporation, more will need to be added regularly to maintain the pond at a proper level. Although you can add water manually as needed, it is better to install an automatic float valve. When the water level drops, the valve will automatically top off the pond. The valve should be located near an area of high water agitation, such as a waterfall, which will aerate new water as it is added and disperse any carbon dioxide.

It is important to note that some water evaporation is normal in a pond. However, should you notice excessive water replacement to the pond, it may indicate there is a leak or a loose connection in the filter system. In such instances, you will need to check fittings, the pond itself, waterfall areas, and so on.

# Protecting Koi from Predators

A pond is a habitat that will inevitably attract wildlife. Although the presence of frogs and other small animals causes only minor problems, some animals can pose a serious danger. Koi spend much time near the water surface and are ready targets for predators, including birds, such as herons and kingfishers, and mammals such as raccoons, foxes, cats, and badgers. Small juvenile koi and fry can easily be eaten by frogs and snakes.

Depending on its location, your pond can also attract birds. Small birds such as sparrows are inconsequential. However, large predators such as herons and kingfishers can empty a pond of fish in no time at all. Kingfishers are particularly adept, setting a routine to feed on the smaller and medium-sized specimens in your koi collection. Once they have located the pond, they will return on a regular basis.

As a general rule, ponds should incorporate

═══ TIP ═══

## Slopes and Shelves

Make sure the sides of the pond go down at a steep angle. Do not allow a gradual slope from the marginal shelves. If the shelves are used for pots of water plants, place the pots close together.

some means of preventing predators from getting near or into the pond. Providing deep-water areas and covering portions of the pond with a monofilament mesh stretched tightly over the pond, about 1 foot (30 cm) above the surface, should prevent most animals from getting to the fish. Electrical fences can also be installed around the perimeter of the pond and activated in the evenings.

*Common predators of koi include kingfishers, herons, weasels, and raccoons.*

*A waterfall is a desirable pond feature, which provides water circulation and aeration.*

*Attractive pond landscapes require careful planning.*

*The use of water lilies and overhanging stone helps provide partial shade for the pond throughout the day.*

*Some type of supplementary aeration should be provided in all ponds to facilitate gas exchange. This pond uses a simple fountain to agitate the pond water.*

*Ponds should be located away from large trees since developing roots can eventually erode and crack walkways and pond structure.*

Installation is relatively simple, provided all the materials and tools are available prior to installation. Such ponds can easily be installed over a weekend; the pond plantings and edging can be completed later.

## Pond Shape and Location

The first step is to decide on the location and desired shape of the pond. Several sketches can be made to help you decide on a pond shape. A rope or a garden hose can then be placed on the ground to help you visualize the selected shape. Once you are satisfied, mark the pond perimeter with stakes or secure the rope in place as a guide when you excavate for the pond.

Ponds can be circular, oval, or kidney-shaped. It is best to stay with a simple standard shape. Complicated designs will make installation of the liner much more difficult, possibly requiring you to weld several liners together. However, the welding process is not that difficult, provided you consult your pet store or garden center about the correct adhesive.

## Determining the Pond Depth

Determine the required pond depth and the depth of any shelf areas you wish to have around the perimeter for plant containers. Then estimate the required size of the liner, allowing an extra amount of material—at least 12 to 14 inches (30.5–35.5 cm) for an overhang. Your garden center or pet store can advise you on the correct-size liner to purchase—simply provide them with the correct measurements.

## Excavating for the Pond

Excavate the soil from the designated area, removing any stones, rocks, or debris that could cause punctures to the liner. If you are going to have a marginal shelf for marsh plants, start by using a shallow excavation for the shelf. Make the shelf approximately 9 to 10 inches (22.9–25 cm) wide and 8 to 10 inches (20–25 cm) below the water's surface.

Closely inspect the pond bottom and sides for jagged stones. If large roots from a nearby tree are found during the excavation, the area may not be the best site for the pond. Always use a carpenter's level to make sure that the pond shelves are horizontal. It is recommended that you dig several inches deeper than the desired depth since a layer of sand will be placed on the bottom.

*A rope or a garden hose is useful for determining the desired size and shape of a pond. Use a carpenters level frequently during pond excavation.*

# POND LINER

## Pond Bottom Preparation

The bottom of the pond as well as the marginal shelf areas will require a layer of sand to protect the pond liner from being damaged. After filling any holes, simply add a layer of sand to the pond bottom and the shelf areas to a depth of approximately 1 to 2 inches (2.5–5 cm) to cushion the liner. Smoothe and firm down the sand layer. Check again for any stones or materials and make a final check of the pond with a level. If using an EPDM liner cushioning material underlay, you will need to install the underlay over the sand prior to installation of the liner. Depending on the type of soil you are using, a layer of sand may not be needed prior to installing the underlay. You should check with your local pond material supplier.

## Installing the Liner

Prior to installation, the pond liner should be warmed in order to make it easier to place In the pond. This is done by unfolding or unrolling the liner and allowing it to lie in the sunlight for 20 to 30 minutes (depending on the outside temperature).

Install the pond liner, draping it loosely but fitting it to the contours of the pond. It is best to have the help of at least one or two other people to install the liner properly. Secure the liner around the pond perimeter with heavy stones. If required, you can fold and pleat the liner to fit into tight corners. Check the perimeter of the pond to ensure that it is level. Add soil underneath the liner and level again if necessary. Fill the pond with water, adding water slowly, a few inches at a time.

## Completing the Installation

When the pond is full, trim any excess liner from the edges, but leave at least 6 to 8 inches (15–20 cm) of excess, which can be covered

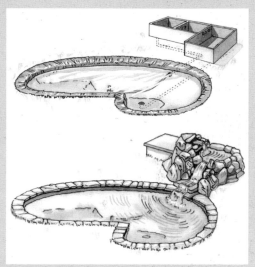

*Secure the pond edge with flagstone or rock, and complete the preparations for the filter system. The finished pond is now ready for the introduction of koi.*

with stone. An edging of flagstone or rock can now be added to finish the pond perimeter.

If a large amount of materials have fallen into the pond during installation, drain the pond water and then refill. This is particularly important if you have used cement to join rocks or stones for the pond edging.

Once the pond has been installed it is now ready for the last steps. The water will need to be conditioned by the addition of a multipurpose water conditioner to remove any chloramines or chlorine that can be toxic to the fish. The filtration connections and installation will need to be completed along with a thorough checking of the system to make sure it is operating properly. If you are adding plants to the pond, you can do this once you have been assured everything else is operating properly. The last step, of course, will be the addition of your pond fish.

# AQUATIC PLANTS AND ALGAE CONTROL

*Aquatic plants not only beautify a koi pond but also serve a multitude of other purposes: They provide some shade for the koi, aid in water purification, and remove nutrients that can encourage the growth of troublesome green algae.*

Aquatic plants provide hiding places for koi, especially juveniles, and provide areas for spawning. Koi attach their eggs to plants during the spring breeding season.

Of the various types of aquatic plants suitable for use in koi ponds, water lilies, pond lilies, and lotuses are particularly recommended. Koi will generally leave lilies alone when they are properly planted and protected. Selection of plants will also depend on the geographical area in which you live. You should consult with a local nursery that supplies aquatic plants for information on selection and care.

With such a large variety of plants to choose from one can either purchase too many plants or not enough. For the pond itself, it is important to consider plant density as well as to

*Water lilies available in various colors make an excellent addition to any pond.*

understand the growing habit of each plant. It is important to space plants out in the pond to allow them enough room to grow properly.

## Containers

Plants should not be planted in soil placed directly in the pond, but planted in tubs filled with a recommended soil mixture. Various types of containers are commercially available for use in the pond environment. They are made from several types of materials, including plastic, clay, and wood.

Using containers in the pond offers several advantages. They can be moved easily whenever you wish, such as during pond cleaning, or to take advantage of the best area and water depths for the plants.

Fertilizers must be kept to a minimum to prevent excessive addition of nitrogen and

### Fertilizers

Some of the best fertilizers for use in feeding aquatic plants are made in the form of sticks or coated beads that can be placed into the soil around the plant. They slowly release nutrients directly to the plant.

phosphates to the water. Bog plants, however, require refertilization every month.

# Basic Plant Categories

Water plants are traditionally divided into three categories: floating plants, shallow-water bog or marsh plants, and submerged plants. A variety of these are readily available from garden centers and through mail-order catalogs.

## Floating Plants

There are are two categories of floating plants: free-floaters, which have roots hanging freely in the water, and attached floaters, whose leaves float on the surface but whose roots are attached to the bottom. Floating plants are easy to care for and are efficient natural water filters, removing large quantities of nitrogen, phosphate, and other substances from the water. They compete with algae for nutrients, thereby minimizing the chance of algal overgrowths.

## Marsh and Bog Plants

Plants that grow in shallow water, with most of the plant above the surface, are included in this category. Many produce vegetation that is quite lush and varied. Bog plants grown in pots and scattered along marginal areas are beautiful additions to the pond. Popular plants include the arrowhead plant (*Sagittaria latifolia*), umbrella plant (*Cyperus alternifolius*), pickerel weed (*Pontederia cordata*), water iris (*Iris* spp.), sweet flag (*Acorus calamus*), and horsetail (*Equisetum hyemale*).

*Pond plants have different water depth requirements. To assure their proper growth, follow the instructions given for the preferred depths. The level of the containers can be adjusted using either concrete blocks or bricks. Water lilies must not be planted too deeply. Bog plants should only be submerged for several inches. Always remember to add a sufficient amount of small pebbles on the top of newly planted vegetation to discourage koi from rooting around in the container and releasing sediments into the pond.*

*A carefully designed marginal shelf permits beautiful landscaping of the pond border. In the deeper areas, various species of water plants including water lilies (*Nymphaea spp.*), lotus (*Nelumbo spp.*), and water poppies (*Hydrocleys nymphoides*) can be placed. The bog section is separated from the main pond by rocks, which allow some water to flow into the area creating a marshy environment. Plants such as the arrowhead (*Sagittaria latifolia*), water iris (*Iris spp.*), and cattails (*Typha spp.*) should do well in a properly maintained bog.*

## Submerged Plants

Submerged plants are rooted on the bottom, with their leaves totally below the surface. These plants are often sold for use in freshwater aquariums and have a high capacity to remove nutrients such as nitrate from the water. They also remove carbon dioxide extremely well and produce an abundance of oxygen into the water; therefore they are often referred to as oxygenating plants. Common examples include *Cabomba, Elodea,* and *Ludwigia.* Care must be taken in using these plants in ponds as they can be quickly uprooted and eaten by koi.

# Popular Plants for Koi Ponds

### Free-Floating Plants

**Water hyacinth** (*Eichornia crassipes*): A tropical floating plant popular with pond owners, it is perennial in warm regions. Best treated as an annual in most of North America, it may also be taken indoors for overwintering in colder climates. The plant has dark green leaves with bulbous bases and bears compact stalks of blue or purple flowers. The short, trailing roots form a compact mass beneath the plant. One of its advantages as a floating pond plant is that it is an excellent natural filter, removing large quantities of nitrogen from water. Water hyacinths do best in full sun.

**Water lettuce** (*Pistia stratiotes*): This attractive floating plant forms rosette-shaped, compact leaf clusters, with a trailing, somewhat compact mass of roots. The plant is equally adaptable to sunny or shady areas of the pond. The plant occurs widely in the tropics, and under favorable conditions reproduces vigorously.

### Attached Floating Plants

**Water lilies** (*Nymphaea* spp.): Undoubtedly the most popular of all aquatic plants, water

*This large koi pond uses water lilies and a variety of marginal plants.*

*A koi pond in Athens, Georgia, with plantings of water lilies, water poppies, and arrowhead.*

*The lotus (*Nelumbo spp.*) produces large, fragrant blooms.*

lilies provide a beautiful covering of leaves and a profusion of flowers. (Sometimes the related yellow pond lily—*Nuphar lutea*—is also called a water lily.) Both tropical and hardy varieties are commonly available for koi ponds. Tropical varieties must either be treated as annuals or taken indoors for overwintering in most of North America; hardy varieties can be left to overwinter outdoors. The lilies can either be planted in pots set on the pond bottom or placed in floating baskets. Water lilies require at least six hours of sunlight per day.

**Lotus** (*Nelumbo* spp.): One of the oldest cultivated water plants, lotuses bear some resemblance to water lilies, but they are in fact unrelated. The plants produce large leaves, often more than 18 inches (45.7 cm) in diameter, and large flowers. During the growing period, the lotus first produces floating leaves that are followed by aerial leaves. The blooms are large, and often very fragrant.

Generally, lotuses are suitable only for large koi ponds due to their rapid growth rate and

*The water poppy,* **Hydrocleys nymphoides,** *grows quickly and produces attractive yellow flowers.*

*Some species of water lilies are night bloomers, opening their blossoms only during the early evenings.*

# CHECKLIST

## Algal Blooms

Major factors that initiate algal blooms are:

1. High concentration of nutrients.
2. Full exposure of pond to sunlight.
3. Inadequate filtration.
4. Lack of water movement.
5. High pH.
6. High temperatures.

their large leaves that can cover the surface of small ponds. However, miniature varieties more suitable for smaller ponds have been developed. Like tropical water lilies, most lotuses need to be moved indoors during the winter season in colder climates. They can do well in cold as long as the water is deep enough to protect the growing portion from freezing. In regions of extreme cold, the pots can be taken in for storage after the leaves have died.

**Note:** Store the pots in a cool area until spring, keeping the soil slightly moist.

**Water poppy** (*Hydrocleys nymphoides*): A popular water plant, water poppies produce abundant oval green leaves and yellow flowers. They are capable of growing quickly and covering the water surface.

## Shallow-water Bog or Marsh Plants

**Umbrella plant** (*Cyperus alternifolius*): Attractive tropical plants that thrive well in shallow pond environments, these plants are characterized by long, umbrella-like leaves at the end of long stems. In cold-weather climates, the plants must be brought inside for the winter.

**Water iris** (*Iris* spp): There are several species of water iris that are excellent for ponds. Irises have swordlike leaves ranging in color from light to dark green, and bear white, yellow, or blue flowers, depending on the species. They are best planted in wooden tubs or pots, submerged to cover the crown of the plant by several inches.

The Japanese water iris (*Iris kaempferi*) is a favorite among pond owners. It has foliage up to 4 feet (1.22 m) in length. Blossoms in various colors, including violet, purple, white, and blue, are produced in late May through June. These plants will thrive in either full sun or partial shade.

The purple water iris (*Iris laevigata*) produces deep-blue flowers with white markings. It also thrives in sun or partial shade, and blooms from spring to fall.

**Horsetail** (*Equisetum hyemale*): This plant is popular for use as a marginal plant. It produces slender, hollow, dark green stems with circular dark rings. It is a fast-growing plant that does well in partial shade.

# Acquiring New Water Plants

It is important to inspect and disinfect water plants before introduction to the pond to prevent possible transmission of certain fish diseases. Parasites, including microscopic larval forms, may be present on the plants, as well as snails, which can become pests. Many invertebrates also serve as carriers of intermediate stages of parasites.

**Aluminum sulfate:** This is a common disinfectant. A working solution is made by dissolving 1 teaspoon per quart (5 cc/L) of water and immersing new plants in the solution for not more than 10 minutes. Remove and rinse well.

The plants can then be safely added to the pond without the fear of introducing parasites.

# Snail Control

Snails are likely to be introduced to the koi pond if plants are not carefully inspected or treated as recommended above. Many snails lay eggs on the plant surfaces, and these will appear as a gelatinous mass. For several reasons, snails are not desirable in koi ponds. Once established, they are quite prolific and can undergo a population explosion. In addition, they destroy aquatic vegetation, preferring to eat the young, tender shoots of many plants. Finally, they can act as vectors for various diseases.

If snails should inadvertently be introduced to your pond, they can be killed with various commercial products.

**Note:** Many of these products contain copper as the active ingredient. Any copper-containing compound may harm both fish and plants!

# Algae Control

Algae growth is one of the most common and annoying situations affecting pond owners. In the natural environment it is normal for algae to increase in early spring. As the season progresses, natural ponds clear on their own. Of course, such ponds are constantly being fed with a fresh supply of water that dilutes the nutrients that encourage algal growth. In any koi pond it is normal to have some algae growing on the bottom and sides of the pond. There are some advantages to this. Algae prevent the buildup of nutrients such as nitrate that normally accumulate in the pond water. They supply accessory oxygen during the day as a by-product of photosynthesis, and also serve as an additional food source for your pond fish.

Algae become troublesome when pond conditions favor a population explosion. Rapid multiplication of algae depletes essential trace elements required by vascular aquatic plants such as water lilies.

## Algae Types

There are two types of algae, differentiated by their growth habits.

**Phytoplanktonic:** *Pelagic* algae are single-celled microscopic plants that live suspended in the water. They prefer to concentrate in the upper portions of the water, where the temperature is higher and they are exposed to more sunlight. Their presence imparts a noticeable green color to water. This type is largely responsible for algal blooms in ponds. Various species can cause blooms, including *Palmella*, *Oscillatoria*, and *Anaebaena*.

**Benthic algae:** These are generally attached to the pond bottom, though some forms can detach and float to the surface, where they form mats. Common types include the waternet, *Hydrodictyon reticulatum*, and the horsehair algae, *Pithophora oedogonia*. Under conditions of low light and high nitrate concentrations a layer of brown algae can develop on the pond surfaces.

# TIP

## Tap Water

If you are using tap water, it has probably been treated with chlorine or chloroamine. You will need to use water conditioners to destroy these toxic chemicals.

*The water hyacinth,* **Eichornia crassipes,** *is a popular floating pond plant. It is also an excellent natural filter because it removes nutrients from the water.*

This indicates the presence of small microscopic algae called diatoms, another nuisance algae.

Prevention is always preferred to using chemicals to control algal blooms. Understanding the causes of algal blooms can help to minimize or prevent serious pond problems.

**Nutrients:** Nutrients are, of course, required for algal growth and reproduction. Nitrogen and phosphorus are especially important. Accelerated algal growth rates correlate with high concentrations of inorganic nitrogen such as ammonia and nitrate. In koi ponds with excess amounts of decaying materials that decompose into ammonia, algae rapidly absorb inorganic nitrogen. This results in a rapid population explosion—an algal bloom.

Aquatic plants are also highly efficient in the uptake of phosphorus. Overfeeding, allowing sediments to build up in ponds, and runoff from adjacent lawns all contribute to the buildup of both nitrogen and phosphorus.

**Light exposure:** Ponds exposed to full sunlight for the entire day will often experience algal blooms. On the other hand, ponds that are located in areas of partial shade seldom have this problem.

**Filtration and water movement:** As mentioned previously, koi ponds should always be equipped with a filtration system. A properly functioning system purifies the water, removing toxic nitrogen compounds such as ammonia. Still pond water favors the growth of algae. Good water movement and aeration can be provided by using a fountain or waterfall. Good water movement in ponds keeps water temperatures more uniform and discourages algae growth.

**High pH and temperature:** Several water parameters are known to be instrumental in favoring algal growth, the most important being pH and temperature. It is known from extensive research that various species of algae, notably blue-green types, favor water with a higher pH because various nutrients, such as phosphorus, are more readily utilized when the water is alkaline. As for temperature, the warmer the water the faster the algae will grow.

## Preventing Algal Blooms

In general, algal blooms can be prevented if specific recommendations are followed in the initial design of the koi pond. If algal blooms do occur, several solutions are available.

The first thing to do is to reduce the nutrient and algae load immediately by changing the water. Slowly add water to the pond, while allowing excess water to drain off until the pond water clears. The addition of water must be slow enough to prevent temperature or pH shock to the fish. However, this will provide only a temporary solution. You will need to find and correct the factors that produced the situation in the first place (such as reducing the amount of sunlight on the pond, increasing the number of vascular plants, decreasing the number of fish).

You may also want to consider the addition of an ultraviolet sterilizer (UV) to your pond's filter system. These water purification devices can be expensive and require maintenance, but they will do an excellent job of preventing algal blooms and maintaining crystal clear water. It is important to make sure that the correct wattage and flow rate are provided for your pond system. Various manufacturers of UV systems can provide you with the type of system that will be best for your pond.

## Algicides

Numerous commercial products are available for treatment of ponds. Approved products sold in the United States are registered with the Environmental Protection Agency (EPA). It is important to follow the instructions on the product carefully. Improper application of algicides can damage or kill tropical plants such as water lilies.

Under most circumstances, use of algicides is not recommended. The decomposing algae increase the demand for oxygen in the pond, and deoxygenation can result in fish mortality.

*Factors responsible for algal blooms include high nutrient concentrations, inadequate filtration, stagnant water, lack of shade, elevated water temperatures, and high pH.*

**Simizine:** A common algicide used for the control of algae is 2-chloro-4, 6-bis-(ethyl-amino)-s-triazine, commonly marketed as Simizine. It is sold under various tradenames.

**Note:** Simizine should be used only during early spring, before the onset of an algae bloom. Care should be exercised to ensure that treated water is not permitted to be used for irrigation, as it will kill plants other than algae.

**Potassium permanganate:** One of the oldest pond algicides, this is rarely used to control algal blooms. However, the chemical is still sold under various trade names. With the advent of better and safer algicides, potassium permanganate products are no longer recommended.

**Important note:** Algicides should be used only when all other means of algae control have failed. The reoccurrence of excessive algae indicates some malfunction in the koi pond design or deterioration of water quality.

# HOW–TO: PLANTING WATER

### Lilies

Water lilies, either tropical or hardy types, should be planted in pots to protect them from being eaten by koi during their initial growing period. After selecting the container, add soil to fill about two-thirds or slightly less. Do not use commercially available potting soils, as these often contain large amounts of peat moss and other ingredients that will float to the pond surface. Ask for a mix that has been formulated for water lilies.

If you are planting tropical water lilies, place the lily root in the center of the container. If you are planting hardy water lilies, it is recommended that you plant them at the edge of the pot with the growing crown facing the opposite edge. Add fertilizer sticks or tablets around the roots, making sure that these do not come into contact with the root. Cover the root with soil, packing down to hold it in place. The growing portion of the lily (crown) should remain above the water surface. Add enough small pea-sized gravel, about ⅓ to ½ inch (8.5–12.7 mm), to fill the pot to the brim. This discourages the koi from digging around in the pot while the plant is establishing itself.

### Water

The next step is to saturate the soil with water, being careful not to disturb the top layer of gravel. Then carefully lower the pot into the water and allow it to rest on the pond bottom. The lily's crown should not be deeper than 6 to 12 inches (15.2–30.5 cm). If necessary, you can place concrete blocks under the pot to maintain the plant at the acceptable water depth. Do not be concerned if some of the leaves are a few inches below the surface. They will reach the surface after a few days. Tropical varieties must be moved indoors to overwinter in temperate areas.

Depending on the health of the plant and prevailing water conditions, it will take approximately three to four weeks for the plants to become acclimated and begin actively growing.

Lilies prefer water with as little disturbance as possible. They do well in areas with some movement but should not be placed in zones of continual water turbulence, such as near filters or aerators.

### Lotuses

Lotuses are planted in a manner similar to water lilies. Using a water-lily mix, add soil until the container is about half full, or slightly less. Place the lotus tuber in the center of the container. Add several fertilizer sticks or tablets, but make sure the fertilizer does not come into contact with the tuber. Cover with soil, packing it down to keep the tuber in place. The crown should be above the soil surface. Add enough small, pea-sized gravel, ⅓ to ½ inch (8.5–12.7 mm) in diameter, to fill to the top of the pot.

*Carefully plant the lily in the soil, making sure you do not cover the crown. Then add a layer of pea-sized gravel.*

# LILIES AND LOTUSES

## Water Again

Saturate the soil with water and lower the pot carefully into the water, allowing it to rest on the pond bottom. The ideal water depth will be 6 to 12 inches (15–30 cm). As with lilies you can place concrete blocks underneath the pot to maintain the plant at an acceptable depth.

Lotuses, like lilies, prefer water with as little disturbance as possible. In addition, they will require fertilization (a few coated beads will be sufficient) at least once monthly.

It is important to note that lotus have a tendency to grow very quickly in ponds. The proper placement of the plants is important. Always allow sufficient room around the plants to allow for the gradual spreading of the leaves. Because lotus do not like water disturbances, keep them away from any water turbulence, such as areas of fountains or areas of waterfalls. And, as a general rule, use the traditional lotus in large ponds and the miniature varieties in smaller ponds. It is also perfectly acceptable to mix various varieties if you have an ample-sized pond.

During the first several weeks after adding lotus (as well as water lilies) to your new pond, make sure you do careful inspections to make sure that they are becoming established successfully. Young plants may need to be protected from koi using wire mesh around the base of the pots if you notice that the young tender leaves are being eaten. Also, during this

*Place the container in the pond, raising it up to the proper water depth with bricks or concrete blocks.*

time, inspect the leaves for any possible insect infestation. If you do notice a yellowing of more than normal numbers of leaves, you will need to carefully inspect the plants for insect pests. If a problem is found, the plants will need to be treated. You can check with your water garden dealer for acceptable treatments for aquatic plants infested with insects.

**Note:** Various types of insecticides are available to safely treat water plants infested with insects. It is always important to make sure that you read all of the precautions on the instructions and to make sure that the product is safe to use in ponds with fish.

# FILTRATION AND POND-WATER QUALITY

*A properly functioning filtration system is required in order to maintain optimal water quality of the koi pond. Although it is possible to maintain a koi pond without a filter system, this could present serious water quality problems in the long term.*

## Filtration Systems

It is essential for koi pond owners to understand the types of filtration and how they function in a pond. Depending on their design, pond filtration systems can be divided into three general categories: closed, semiclosed, and open.

**Closed pond systems:** These systems are defined as those in which the water is recirculated and purified by filter devices. Closed systems utilize biological filtration, supplemented with chemical and mechanical methods. Such systems rely primarily on the filter devices to maintain water quality, with additional water added as needed to replace loss to evaporation.

**Semiclosed systems:** These utilize a means of minimal filtration, but are supplemented by the

*A beautiful pond in San Jose, California, equipped with both a biological filter and a UV sterilizer system.*

constant, regulated addition of fresh water. Semiclosed pond systems are uncommon, primarily due to the cost of constantly adding water. In addition, the new water must be treated before addition to the pond to detoxify harmful chemicals such as chlorine.

**Open systems:** Open systems are those in which the water is purified by the constant addition of new water and draining of the old—much like a natural pond fed by a stream.

## Filtration Processes

The actual processes by which water is cleaned in recirculation systems are classified into three types: *biological, mechanical,* and *chemical.* All three play an important role in contributing to good water quality. Ideally, closed systems should utilize all of these methods to maintain maximum water quality, clarity, and carrying capacity.

# Biological Filtration

Biological filtration is the most important cleansing process in ponds and other aquatic systems. It is carried out by specific bacteria, through the chemical processes of nitrification and denitrification. While they are also found suspended in the water, the majority of these bacteria grow in a film (biofilm) that covers the submerged surfaces of the pond.

## Understanding the Nitrogen Cycle

Nitrogen is used by organisms for the synthesis of proteins and other compounds. Most organisms cannot use nitrogen gas directly from the air, but must obtain it in a combined form.

When organic matter decays, its proteins are broken down by bacteria. Among the products are ammonia. Ammonia is also released through a fish's gills as a metabolic waste product. The accumulation of ammonia in a pond is a serious problem as it is toxic to fish in low concentrations. Fortunately, once in the water, ammonia is utilized as an energy source by several types of *nitrifying* bacteria. *Nitrosomonas* chemically transforms ammonia into less toxic nitrites. *Nitrobacter* utilizes nitrites as an energy source, converting them into less toxic nitrates. In this form they can be utilized by plants, which turn them back into protein. Some of the nitrate is converted by *denitrifying* bacteria into free nitrogen, which rises in bubbles to the top of the pond and is released back into the atmosphere.

While in a pond system the nitrification process occurs most intensively within the filter, the bacteria that mediate the nitrogen cycle are present in virtually every part of the pond, including plant surfaces, pond sides, and debris.

## Types of Biological Filters

Biological filters generally utilize sand and gravel layers as the filter media. Bacteria attach to the gravel grains and perform the necessary purification. It should be emphasized that the surface area of a filter is very important. The greater the surface area, the larger the population of nitrifying bacteria it can support, and the greater the *carrying capacity*, or the number of fish that can be maintained in the koi pond. For that reason alone, small submerged-type pond box filters sold for use in ponds are often inadequate as filters for a koi pond.

Although their actual appearance can vary according to the manufacturer or designer, fil-

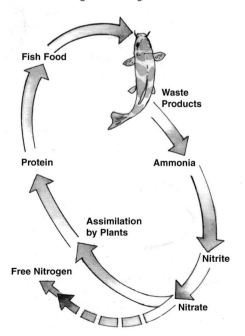

Fish Food

Waste Products

Protein

Ammonia

Assimilation by Plants

Nitrite

Free Nitrogen

Nitrate

*Biological filtration, accomplished through the nitrogen cycle, is principally carried out by bacteria in the filter bed.*

*Various types of filters can be used for the koi pond: biological filters (top and left); sand pressure filters (right).*

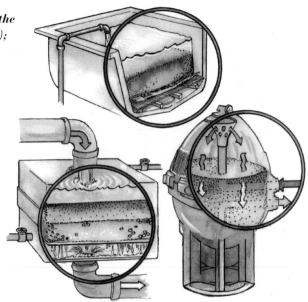

tration systems can be divided into two major types: inside filters that are placed in the pond, and outside filters.

Though there are many designs, all operate in a similar manner.

**Inside biological filters:** These filters are often used in smaller ponds, and can be as simple as a small box holding filter media and a pump. Though they do a fair job of mechanical debris removal in smaller ponds, they are not as efficient as outside systems in providing optimal biological purification. Smaller filters perform best when the carrying capacity (or *bioload*) of the system is low.

The major problem with such filters is that they clog easily.

**Outside biological filters:** These filters are the most popular systems. When designed correctly they can be very efficient and can be conveniently located perhaps concealed behind shrubs or trees. The filter is connected to the pond using a combination of intake and outlet pipes. Water is removed through a bottom drain and from several other areas of the pond, routed to the filter where it is purified, and returned to the pond through an aerating device such as a fountain or a waterfall. The filter can be either a gravity-fed or a reverse-flow type. Both can yield good results.

The advantage of outside filters is that they automatically remove debris and pollutants from the pond. Sediments and debris accumulate in the filter where they can then be

removed through use of backwash systems (reversing the flow to remove trapped particles and debris). Such filters also are very easy to maintain. The surface of the filter need only be raked on occasion to break up the formation of algae. This prevents channeling.

## TIP

### Adding Chemicals

Under no circumstances should any medications or chemicals be added to the koi pond during the conditioning period. Some of these substances are known to either inhibit or prevent the development of filter-bed bacteria. Chemicals containing methylene blue or erythromycin particularly affect the growth of filter-bed bacteria adversely.

*The clarity of this pond is achieved through the use of a properly designed and maintained filter system.*

## Selecting Filter Media

Selection of the proper shape and size of the gravel or other substrate is necessary for proper filter bed functioning. Size-graded gravel is the most common type of medium used in filter-beds. As most of the nitrifying activity is concentrated in the top layer of the filter, smaller-sized particles are used there to increase the available surface area. However, the grain size must not be so small as to prevent proper water circulation through the bed.

In outside biological filters, various types of gravel and rock should be layered. The total filter bed should be approximately 2 to 3 feet (61–91.4 cm) in depth. The topmost layer will be composed of fine gravel, gradually enlarging to large pebbles, small rocks, and large rocks. Generally, gravel grains of ⅛ to ¼ inch (3–6 mm) are recommended for the top layer. There should be an undergravel substrate of at least 12 inches (30.5 cm) on the plate. Properly constructed, such a bed will allow proper percolation and backwashing of the filter.

**Alternative substrates:** With the advent of many new substrate materials, filter beds need not utilize only gravel. Some of these products actually perform better than the classical graded gravels. Filter bacteria are not fussy in their choice of surfaces to grow on. They will attach to gravel, plastic, epoxy, concrete, etc. Various types of lightweight plastic and ceramic "biorings" have been marketed for some time.

## Filter Bed Maintenance

If not overburdened, a properly designed biological filter bed is virtually maintenance free. Occasional backwashing and light raking of the surface to remove trapped debris is all that is necessary. Raking of the top of the filter bed retards the growth of algae, and avoids buildup of sediments and channeling.

Channeling can result when excessive amounts of debris plug the filter. Water then moves through zones of least resistance, forming channels, and leaving portions of the filter devoid of water circulation. This is a potentially dangerous situation.

Since the nitrification process is dependent on oxygen, the blocked areas begin to develop undesirable anaerobic bacteria that produce toxic gases such as methane and hydrogen sulfide, which can harm koi and other aquatic organisms.

## Conditioning

Like aquariums, ponds require conditioning after they are placed in operation. The conditioning period is the time required for nitrifying bacteria to become established on the filter bed of a new pond.

New ponds undergoing conditioning have certain water characteristics, including high ammonia, the presence of nitrite, and a slow increase of nitrate. Once the conditioning period is over, ammonia and nitrite should not be detectable, although nitrate will continue to accumulate as the end product of nitrification.

It is important not to overstock the pond with fish during the conditioning period so as to minimize stress and possible koi mortalities. If the pond is overstocked, the concentration of toxic ammonia will increase, possibly to lethal levels.

The conditioning period requires approximately four to six weeks at temperatures of 75 to 80°F (24–26.5°C).

## Filtration Rates

Water should flow through the filter at a rate that provides slightly more than adequate turnover. The filter size will obviously depend on the size of the pond as well as the rate at which the recirculating pump operates. A general rule of thumb is that water should have a minimum turnover rate through the filter of about 2 to 6 gallons (7.57–22.7 L) per square foot (.093 m$^2$) of filter surface per minute.

*Regular pond maintenance is required to keep ponds in the best condition. This large pond in the city of San Jose, California, receives a thorough spring cleaning to remove any accumulated sediments, as well as to inspect the concrete surfaces for any cracks.*

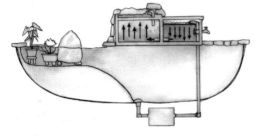

Of course, the rate will need to be adjusted according to the system. Always purchase a pump that allows variable adjustment of the circulation rate. As a general rule, the total volume of water should pass through at least one complete cycle in about two hours.

## Carrying Capacity

Carrying capacity, or *bioload*, is the quantity of fish that a pond can safely sustain once the system has been conditioned. A common mistake is not allowing for the fact that koi grow very quickly. For example, small 3- to 4-inch (7.6–10.2 cm) koi will grow to be 12 inches (30.5 cm) or more within a few years. As they grow they add to the bioload, increasing the daily amount of ammonia and waste products added to the pond. At the point where the filter can no longer handle the waste products generated by the koi, you will either have to add additional filter capacity or reduce the number

*Filtration is important for the proper functioning of koi ponds. Biological filters can be located adjacent to the pond and concealed behind a waterfall or plantings. Care must be used in plumbing the filters to prevent leaks.*

of koi to bring the pond back to its carrying capacity. Therefore, it is better to plan ahead by carefully considering the initial number of koi.

Add one 10-inch (25.4-cm) fish for every 20 square feet (1.86 m sq) of pond surface area. For example, a pond with dimensions of 10 x 20 feet (3.05 x 6.1 m) would be 200 square feet (18.6 m sq). With proper filtration and aeration, the pond could accommodate a maximum of 10 koi, each 10 inches (25.4 cm) long. One must bear in mind that this is a very conservative figure. Ponds that utilize maximal filtration rates, have good aeration, have stable water temperatures, and ensure frequent water changes could safely accommodate additional fish. On the other hand, ponds with marginal filtration, overfeeding, infrequent water changes, poor aeration, high water temperatures, and algal problems may not be able to sustain the recommended amount of healthy fish safely.

## Mechanical Filtration

Mechanical filtration is the process of removing suspended particulate matter from water. This function is performed by the filter sand in which debris is trapped. The filter sand can either be inside or outside the pond.

Because excess accumulation plays a role in development of certain disease organisms, the reduction of particulate matter in koi ponds is extremely important. Particulate matter includes uneaten food, plant materials, fecal waste, and dead organisms. Eventually the material settles as sediment on the pond bottom, where it can be stirred up when disturbed by the fish.

In many situations only a biological filter will be needed. In koi ponds with large numbers of koi, numerous plants, and low water movement, however, an accessory system is highly recommended to pre-filter particulate matter from the water prior to its passage through the biological filter bed.

### Pressurized Sand Filters

For large koi ponds, the use of pressurized sand filters makes the job of removing suspended particles from the water easy. These are the same type of filters used to clarify swimming pools. They utilize fine sand as a substrate, have a high turnover rate, and are capable of efficiently removing particulate matter. Keep in mind that they are purely mechanical and perform little, if any, biological filtration.

Pressurized sand filters require some routine maintenance, and it is imperative that they be backwashed on a regular schedule. Some models have a built-in setting that will backwash automatically on a preset schedule. Generally, mechanical filters should not be used without additional biological filtration.

## Chemical Filtration

Chemical filtration is the removal of dissolved organic and inorganic compounds by adhesion onto porous substrates or by chemical processes such as air stripping, ozonation, and ultraviolet light.

Various chemicals, originating from various biological activities, accumulate in water. These pollutants often give water a yellowish appearance. The chemicals in question include proteins, fats, amino acids, and other organics. Evidence continues to accumulate concerning the deleterious effects of some of these chemicals on fish. In the majority of cases removal is accomplished by making regular water changes each month and/or by the use of special substances such as activated carbon.

### Activated Carbon

This is an effective chemical filtrant that removes various pollutants as well as detergents and insecticides. Although the constant use of activated carbon is generally unnecessary in ponds, it can be employed to reduce the concentration of undesirable pollutants. It is particularly useful for removing medications and chemicals from water after treatment has been completed.

Consult your local garden shop or pond retailer for more information on selecting carbons for use in pond filters.

### Ultraviolet Sterilizers

Ultraviolet sterilizers are employed extensively in larger tropical aquarium systems such as those used in public aquariums. In the past they were not commonly used in ponds, but have been incorporated in ponds more frequently over past years. This is due in part to the manufacture of sterilizer units specifically built for pond usage. They are excellent for larger systems where they will optimize water clarity. Ultraviolet sterilizers are capable of reducing the number of bacteria, parasites, and phytoplanktonic algae. In general, ultraviolet sterilizers can be considered optional equipment and are not a requirement for the successful operation of a koi pond.

# WATER QUALITY AND ANALYSIS

*This chapter provides an overview of various water-quality parameters and how they help to provide a proper environment for koi.*

Once a koi pond is functioning it will be important to carefully monitor the water quality, especially during the first month of operation. Monitoring of the water can easily be done using various types of water test kits.

## Water-Quality Parameters

Several major changes come into play once the system is set into operation, including a rise in ammonia, nitrite and nitrate concentrations, an increase in phosphates, and a decline in pH.

These changes necessitate a program of regular water-quality monitoring of your koi pond. The diligent monitoring of water quality will ensure long-lived and healthy fish.

### Temperature

Temperature tolerances vary according to the species of fish. Koi are a very hardy species, tolerant of temperature changes and fluctua-

*A well-established pond with water lilies and lush marginal plantings.*

tions. Nevertheless, a range of 68 to 75°F (20.0–23.9°C) is recommended, especially during the summer season. Gradual change from one temperature to another is also recommended.

### Dissolved Oxygen

Oxygen that is dissolved in the water (DO) is in great demand in koi ponds and other aquatic systems. It is consumed by fish and plants in respiration, and is utilized in various chemical processes, including bacterial decomposition in the nitrogen cycle. The amount of dissolved oxygen required is referred to as biological oxygen demand (BOD). The filter bed is a heavy user of oxygen.

The solubility of oxygen in water is dependent on several factors, including temperature, salinity, and agitation. In freshwater systems, the effect of salinity is negligible.

Temperature inversely affects oxygen solubility. The higher the temperature, the lower the DO level. As the oxygen concentration decreases below acceptable levels, koi will react with an increased respiratory rate. As a general rule,

━━━ TIP ━━━

**Preventing pH Shock to Koi**

To prevent pH shock to koi, never attempt to adjust the pH of the pond water unless you have an accurate pH test kit. And never attempt to alter the pH by more than 0.2 units a day.

dissolved oxygen concentrations should be maintained at 5.0 to 5.5 mg per L, at least.

Low dissolved oxygen concentration is often a problem during summer months when water temperatures increase. Low oxygen concentration in koi ponds can also be traced to excess organic materials.

Ample water circulation and agitation are critical in a koi pond. In ponds with poor water agitation, oxygen levels can quickly drop to abnormally low concentrations. The idea is to keep the water surface moving constantly so that oxygen is dissolved properly. The most common methods of agitation involve the use of rock raceways, waterfalls, and fountains.

It is important to note that koi will utilize more oxygen after feeding. If the fish are fed heavily at high water temperatures, the increased oxygen consumption can reduce oxygen levels to dangerously low concentrations.

Dissolved oxygen can also be depleted when heavy growths of algae occur. Algae produce oxygen during the day but utilize oxygen at night, and heavy growth can be a problem.

## Carbon Dioxide

Carbon dioxide is a product of respiration by both plants and animals. In ponds it is dissolved in the water, from which it can be driven off by agitation. High levels of carbon dioxide can severely affect normal respiration, preventing the intake of oxygen, even though ample oxygen may be present.

## pH

Water can be acidic, neutral, or alkaline. The measure of this, referred to as pH, must be monitored regularly.

The pH of pond water decreases naturally over time due to an increase in organic matter and a decrease in the buffering capacity of the water. Koi are quite tolerant of various pH levels. However, it is recommended that the pH not fluctuate too greatly, and not be lower that 6.8 or higher than 8.0. In general, koi prefer alkaline water, 7.0 to 7.8, with 6.8 and 8.0 being the upper and lower limits. Juvenile koi are more sensitive to pH changes than adults. Rapid changes in pH can result in shock.

If the pH is not within recommended ranges, it can be adjusted using commercially available buffers. These will either raise or lower the pH.

## Hardness

Hardness is defined as the amount of calcium and magnesium carbonate present in water. Hardness varies depending on the area of the country. Koi do poorly in extremely hard water, and will not survive in soft water. In addition, soft water has poor buffering capacity—that is to say, it lacks the ability to maintain a stable pH. Moderately hard and very hard conditions are generally associated with buffer compounds. Carbonates and bicarbonates decrease pH decline in pond water.

Hardness is generally expressed in degrees of carbonate hardness (DH) or parts per million

*A colorimetric test kit (top) relies on a change of color in the test sample. The sample is then matched with a set of color standards to determine the concentration of the chemical being tested. Though more precise than a colorimetric kit, an electronic pH meter (center) is more expensive and requires more maintenance. Simple dip stick kits (bottom) are also available.*

(ppm). Water is considered soft if it has a hardness of less than 75 ppm, and hard if within 150 to 300 ppm.

Maintaining proper water hardness can be a serious problem. It should be monitored, especially in areas where the water is soft. Koi prefer moderately hard, alkaline water, in which they appear to have brighter colors.

## Nitrogen Compounds

The accumulation of inorganic nitrogen in ponds can be quite troublesome for the new koi pond owner. Inorganic nitrogen includes ammonia, nitrite, and nitrate. These are generated from the breakdown of organic materials. Accumulation of nitrogen compounds can predispose fish to diseases, reduce normal growth, and damage delicate gills.

**Ammonia:** This is the principal product of the decay of nitrogenous waste. Excreted by koi, principally through their gills as a waste product, it is, as discussed, the most toxic of the nitrogen compounds. Ammonia can be toxic to koi at low concentrations, especially to fry and juvenile fish.

Ammonia readily dissolves in water and exists in two different forms: as toxic free ammonia ($NH_3$) and in the nontoxic ionized form, called ammonium ($NH_4^+$). The percentage of each type is dependent on a number of factors, including pH and temperature. High pH and temperature favor the toxic free ammonia form. The toxicity of ammonia is dependent on various factors, including individual species sensitivity.

Koi are more tolerant of slightly higher concentrations of ammonia than many other fish species.

Excessive concentration of ammonia is an indicator of inefficient biological filtration, overfeeding, overcrowding, and the decomposition of organic material in the pond. If the concentration is above acceptable levels, an immediate water change must be made to prevent mortalities. As a general rule, free ammonia should not exceed 0.036 mg per gallon (0.01 mg/L).

**Nitrite:** Formed from the metabolic conversion of ammonia by *Nitrosomonas* bacteria, nitrite is the ionized form of nitrous acid. While it is less poisonous than ammonia, it can be toxic to koi. High concentrations occur principally during the conditioning period of the biological filter. Typically, when this time is past, nitrite concentrations will be negligible. A continual persistent concentration of nitrite in the pond indicates a problem with the filter.

The toxicity of nitrite is due to its effects on oxygen transport, damage to important compounds in the blood, and direct damage to fish tissue.

**Nitrates:** These are formed from the oxidation of nitrites by bacteria. They are very soluble in water, and are much less toxic than ammonia or nitrite. In pond water, they could become a problem when present in concentrations in excess of 200 ppm (mg/L). Like nitrites, nitrates can affect the intake of oxygen by koi and reduce their normal growth rate.

## Other Toxic Chemicals

Other chemicals that are toxic to koi include chlorine and chloramines, heavy metals, detergents, and insecticides. Caution must be used to prevent the introduction of such compounds into your pond. For example, care must be taken to ensure that insecticides are kept away from the pond. Covering the pond is the best safety measure if garden sprays need to be used in adjacent areas.

**Chlorine and chloramines:** Chlorine and chloramines are commonly used for the disinfection of municipal water. Although treated water is safe for human use, it is unsafe and extremely toxic to fish. Municipal water must be treated with multipurpose water conditioners to remove any chlorine prior to the introduction of any koi or other aquatic animals.

Chloramine can also be present in city water and has recently come into use in most American municipalities, with a continual switch from chlorine to chloramine over the past several years. This compound can be thought of simply as chlorine and ammonia combined. It is even more toxic than elemental chlorine. Tests have shown that as little as 0.05 ppm of chloramine can kill fish. Unlike chlorine-treated water, agitation of the water alone will not dissipate chloramine.

Water that contains chloramines must be treated prior to addition to the koi pond. Chloramines can be detoxified in water by the addition of all-purpose commercial water conditioners that destroy chloramine. An alternative method is to filter water by passing it through activated carbon or an ammonia-reducing zeolite.

For most pond owners, the easiest way to detoxify chloramines is to add a water conditioner to the pond in the area where you add new water, but this method is suitable only when small amounts of water (less than 10 percent of the pond volume) are being replaced, such as in cases of partial water changes, or the replacement of evaporated water. You should note that when chloramines are destroyed they release ammonia into the water. In ponds with inadequate filtration, a temporary rise in ammonia can occur. This should not be a problem in ponds with slightly acidic water and a well-

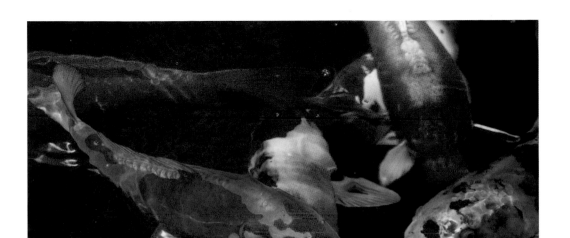

*A thriving collection of koi in a well-monitored and well-maintained pond.*

functioning filter. In alkaline water, however, the ammonia remains in the toxic form. Nevertheless, in well-filtered ponds the ammonia will be rapidly destroyed by the biological-filter-bed bacteria. Consequently, you need not be too concerned when making partial water changes to the pond, or when replenishing water lost by evaporation.

**Heavy metals:** Water can contain traces of copper, lead, aluminum, and zinc, metals that are toxic in low concentrations. Koi pond owners should be aware of the potential problems with these. Heavy metals can be present in city water as well as well water. Older plumbing can contribute substantial amounts of copper, lead, and zinc. Metals can exist in free or chelated form. The harder the water, the less toxic is the metal.

**Warning:** Never use copper piping, fixtures, or equipment in koi ponds.

## Water Analysis

The regular monitoring of water quality in the garden pond is an important part of preventive water maintenance. Some tests should be conducted on a weekly basis while others should be performed monthly.

The frequency of testing is dependent on various factors. Generally, the newer the pond the more frequently the tests should be performed. Once the pond has been conditioned and is in operation for several months, the frequency can be reduced to several times a month, unless you suspect a problem is developing.

# POND CARE
# AND MAINTENANCE

*Established ponds require maintenance to ensure that the pond and water filtration equipment remains in optimal operation. Although well-designed koi pond systems require a minimum of maintenance, there are routine tasks that should be performed throughout the year.*

## Maintenance

Once the koi pond is in operation it will be necessary to perform routine maintenance tasks on a regular schedule. Daily, weekly, monthly, and special spring and winter maintenance of the pond will ensure its continued beauty and quality, at the same time providing a healthy environment for your koi. Ignoring routine maintenance tasks can eventually lead to clogged filters, malfunction of poorly-cared-for equipment, or even disasters such as the sudden draining of the pond due to tears in the pond liner.

In addition to the tasks associated with the pond itself, you should also make a regular examination of your koi to ensure that they are in good health and not developing any

*All ponds need a regular maintenance program to keep them functioning at their best.*

serious disease problems. Generally, the best time to do this is during feeding.

## Seasonal Care

### Fall and Winter

As the weather begins to change in the fall, it signals the upcoming cold temperatures of winter. Pond maintenance during the fall will primarily be in removing any excess leaves that accumulate in the pond, continual water-quality testing, and other basic routine maintenance done in the other seasons. You will also notice that as the temperatures begin to drop, your koi will begin eating less.

The preparations for the winter season vary according to the geographical region. In colder climates, they will include removal of all organic materials and leaves from the pond. Any tropical

*Various tasks like removing leaves from the water, trimming marginal plants, and removing bottom sediments keep ponds like this one operating properly.*

cracks. If cracks are found, the pool will need to be drained completely and thoroughly cleaned prior to any repair work.

If soil and leaves have accumulated on the pond bottom in excess of 1 inch (2.54 cm), it will be necessary to drain the pond and remove this debris. Such a situation is potentially dangerous, since the thick sediment promotes the growth of anaerobic bacteria.

## Examining Your Koi

Koi, like other fish, are cold-blooded animals. Their body temperature is close to the ambient water temperature. The functioning of the fish's immune system is related to temperature. During the winter a koi's physiological function changes dramatically. Respiration decreases, digestion ceases, and the immune system is for the most part nonfunctional.

*A properly designed koi pond will reduce maintenance and avoid the need for costly modifications.*

In the spring, as water temperatures begin to increase, so does the fish's metabolism. The immune system, however, takes longer to become fully functional.

If koi were carrying a bacterial disease, for example, and were introduced to the pond in the fall, the low seasonal temperature would usually inhibit the development of the disease until spring. At that time, the fish will often be unable to fight the infection, since its immune system is not functioning at its capacity.

As the water temperature increases, bacteria in the water are able to grow faster, while the fish's immune system is still depressed. It may become necessary to treat the fish with antibiotics early in the spring as a preventive measure against development of bacterial disease. This will be discussed further in the chapter on diseases (see page 81).

Examination is best accomplished just prior to feedings, when the fish gather at the feeding area. Several aspects of their general behavior should be examined:

✔ Carefully evaluate their swimming abilities and respiration rate.

✔ See if they are scratching themselves on the pond bottom or staying in areas of high water agitation.

✔ Also evaluate their buoyancy, an aspect that is often affected if the fish begins to develop a systemic bacterial disease.

✔ Look for any lesions, including frayed fins, ulcers, abnormal swellings, spots, etc. These could indicate developing bacterial or parasitic disease.

✔ The appearance of any transparent fecal casts in the water is a sign of possible bacterial, viral, or parasitic infections of the gastrointestinal tract.

*A barrier-type net makes it easy to herd koi into sections of the pond for removal during cleaning operations.*

# Pond Cleaning Tasks

As discussed previously, there are various routine tasks that need to be performed in and around a koi pond.

## Equipment

Some basic equipment will need to be acquired in order to perform the basic maintenance chores. This will include several clean buckets, a good-quality fishnet, and a dipping net for skimming off leaves and other debris. A barrier net is also recommended to easily herd koi for removal to temporary holding facilities. A bristle bush with a long handle is necessary for scrubbing the pond bottom and sides to remove excess algae, and a hose-

powered pool vacuum cleaner is also helpful for removing debris from the bottom.

It is important to note that care must be exercised when cleaning ponds with plastic liners. Hard bristles could damage the surfaces. Brushes with soft bristles are therefore recommended.

## Removing Organic Materials

Leaves from surrounding trees or shrubs that have fallen into the pond should be removed on a regular basis. Decaying leaves produce ammonia that can fuel the growth of unwanted algae. Leaves, evergreen needles, and other debris should be removed daily, particularly during the fall season. The severity of this problem is variable, depending on the region in which you live and the types of vegetation adjacent to the pond.

Any koi food remaining in the pond 1 hour after feeding should be removed using a dip net. If left in the pond, it will decay, contributing to the fouling of the pond water. This is far more serious in smaller koi ponds than larger ones.

## Cleaning of Recirculation and Submersible Pumps

Pumps should be inspected regularly, especially during the summer, to make sure they are functioning properly. Both types of pumps will generally require only cleaning of the strainer that traps large particles. You should check the manufacturer's recommendations on maintenance and service of your pond pumps.

## Cleaning Filters

Although there are various types of filters, all will require some maintenance to assure their proper functioning. Sand pressure filters will require backwashing, small submerged pond filters will need to be cleaned, and any activated carbon or other filter materials changed.

Large biological filters will require regular maintenance. It is important to rake the surface of the filter bed every few days, especially in the summer months, to break up any algae growth and to minimize clogging and channeling. Clogged filters function at reduced efficiency, promoting the development of anaerobic bacteria and their toxic waste products.

A garden rake is all that is necessary to perform this maintenance task. Simply draw the rake across the top of the filter surface bed to break up the formation of any clumps of algae. Make sure the rake penetrates the surface to a depth of at least an inch or more.

## Cleaning Excessive Algae from Pond Surfaces

If excessive benthic algae has grown on the pond surfaces, remove it with a brush. This is not to imply that all algae should be removed, as it serves as food for koi. However, in order to maintain an aesthetically pleasing pond, some algae can be removed from the surfaces.

## Changing Water

Once a month some water should be changed in the pond to reduce the buildup of nutrients. Although filters detoxify harmful nitrogen products such as ammonia and nitrite, other chemical components such as nitrate and various organics will remain in the pond water. A recommended solution to this problem is to make partial water changes to the pond to dilute these organics. It is recommended that you change one-third of the volume once

---

**TIP**

### Skimmers

Larger ponds often have overflow setups, or *skimmers*, that collect floating debris and other materials. If your pond has this feature, make sure that the overflow is cleaned daily in the summer and at least weekly during other seasons. The frequency of cleaning is based on prevailing water temperatures and how fast the overflows become filled with debris.

---

every three months. The information you get from water tests will help guide you in setting a schedule for water changes.

## Full Pond Cleaning

Every few years the pond will require a full cleaning. This will depend on the condition of the pond, filter type, and other factors. Full cleaning requires a complete draining of the water. Of course, the koi will have to be removed to a temporary holding area during cleaning and inspection.

Prior to the actual draining of the water, it is important to determine the amount and extent of any debris, such as leaves and sediment, on the pond bottom. If large amounts of debris are present, caution must be used to prevent disturbing the material while the koi are present in the pond. Disturbance of accumulated bottom materials releases toxic substances, reducing the concentration of dissolved oxygen. This reaction occurs quickly, especially in water with high temperatures.

# NUTRITION

*Koi easily feed on a wide variety of both plant and animal foods; however, as with other animals, not all foods are necessarily the best for them. They have specific dietary requirements that need to be met in order to keep them healthy.*

## Nutritional Guidelines

Extensive research has yielded a substantial amount of information about the nutritional requirements of koi. Although pond fish will accept just about any type of food offered, this should not be taken to mean that any type of food is necessarily good for them. There are clear nutritional guidelines that, if followed, will produce healthy, happy fish.

## Nutrition and Disease

Lack of essential nutrients is known to have deleterious effects on the immune system. Koi with impaired immune systems are unable to fight infections properly. Deficiency or excess of certain nutrients can produce noninfectious diseases as well. Providing a good nutritional

*Keeping koi healthy requires an understanding of their nutritional requirements.*

program, with the selection of properly formulated foods, is essential for healthy koi.

## Metabolic Requirements

The nutrients supplied in the daily diet are utilized for various bodily functions. Koi energy requirements are variable, and depend on different factors including the age of the fish, its feeding habits and behavior, and water temperatures. Nutrients are used for growth, tissue repair, daily activity, and other functions as well. Koi will have different energy requirements depending on the stage of their life cycle as well. Younger koi need more calories per day to sustain their rapid growth and higher metabolic needs.

## General Dietary Requirements

Koi require specific amounts of certain components in their diet. The major nutritional groups are protein, lipids (fats), carbohydrates, fiber, and vitamins and minerals.

## Protein

Required for normal physiological function and growth, protein is found in plants, animals, and bacteria. The percentage of protein required varies according to species and age. Generally, the amount of protein in a diet can be reduced as the fish matures. For example, fry and fingerling koi should be fed diets that range from 37 to 42 percent protein. With adults, however, protein can be reduced to 30 to 38 percent. Under no circumstances should koi be fed a steady diet containing less than 30 percent protein, as deficiency will result.

Proteins are composed of smaller units called amino acids. There are 20 amino acids in all, and it has been determined that 10 of them are essential for normal growth and development. A deficiency in any of these essential amino acids results in low weight gain and depressed appetite.

## Lipids

Primarily an energy source, lipids are also a vital component of internal organs and cells. The high lipid content of fish helps them to maintain neutral buoyancy. Collectively, lipids include fats, phospholipids, steroids, and waxes.

Lipids are divided into two chemical categories—saturated and unsaturated. Unsaturates are more easily utilized than the saturates. In fact, too much saturated fat in the diet can have deleterious effects. Therefore, prepared diets that include saturated-fat sources such as pork, beef, or poultry should not be used for feeding koi. On the other hand, diets high in unsaturated fish oils are preferred and are better utilized by koi. Most prepared diets have an acceptable 5 to 8 percent of total fat.

Too much fat in the diet results in excessive weight gain and fatty infiltration of the liver. A deficiency in the essential fatty acids can cause fin erosion, predisposition to shock, and heart degeneration.

It is important that the foods fed to koi should be specially formulated for them.

## Carbohydrates

The majority of prepared foods, such as floating koi pellets, often contain high percentages of carbohydrates. In reviewing the ingredients in these foods you will notice they include various sources of carbohydrates, including wheat, corn, and rice.

In koi and many other fish species, carbohydrates are absorbed slowly as simple sugars. Although koi can utilize carbohydrates, recent research has indicated that they do not digest them as efficiently as once thought. Based on scientific studies, carbohydrates should constitute not more than 30 to 40 percent of the dietary intake. Therefore, diets prepared primarily with cereals (rice, wheat, corn, etc.) should be avoided.

## Fiber

Fiber is the dietary component that is not digested during passage through the fish's intestinal tract. It is believed that fiber aids in digestion and the transit of food through the intestine. Although fiber is a necessary dietary component, excessive amounts can interfere with the absorption of various nutrients and reduce normal growth. Also, the excreted excess can significantly add to the organic debris in the pond. For these reasons high-fiber diets should be avoided. Commercially prepared foods with fiber content below 5 percent are recommended for use.

## Vitamins

Water-soluble vitamins include the B complex and vitamin C. The fat-soluble vitamins are A, D, E, and K. The requirements for vitamins in koi vary, depending on numerous factors including age, size, stress, and prevailing water conditions. Vitamin deficiencies can be particularly serious in young fish.

Vitamin deficiencies result in various disease syndromes. The signs are often nonspecific, but generally, you will notice a decrease in food consumption, with a developing pattern of increased mortalities.

## Minerals

Minerals are required by koi for normal tissue formation, normal metabolism, and osmoregulation (the various physiological processes that maintain the proper balance of salts and water within the fish). Fish obtain their minerals both from their food and directly from the water; however, only a few minerals can be absorbed in sufficient quantities from water. Iron, copper, iodine, magnesium, and others must be supplied in the diet.

Calcium and phosphorus are two important minerals required in large concentrations for normal growth and metabolic function. Koi are able to absorb calcium directly from the water, but they must have adequate concentrations of phosphorus in their diet to absorb the calcium.

A deficiency in dietary phosphate results in slower growth, appetite depression, and the development of deformed heads and backs.

# Koi Food

## Food Types

Koi are omnivorous fish, consuming both animal and plant materials. Various types of food will be accepted by them, including fresh, freeze-dried, and dried preparations. Careful selection of foods from these categories will ensure a healthy dietary regime.

**Fresh food:** Fresh vegetables including lettuce, squash, and others can be fed, but should be considered only as supplementary. Pieces of shrimp, fish, earthworms, and clams are also acceptable as supplements and to supply some variety, but are not required foodstuffs.

**Freeze-dried food:** These foods, such as plankton, fresh water shrimp, daphnia, and tubifex and bloodworms are sometimes used

*Various types of prepared foods are available commercially for feeding koi (clockwise from the top): flake foods, extruded stick foods, and floating pellets.*

*Always feed koi sparingly in ponds to avoid overfeeding and the accumulation of food on the bottom. Excess food can leave nutrients in the water, increasing algae growth, turning a beautiful pond cloudy.*

gest that one shape is better than another. Acceptance of foods by koi is related to the nutritional profile and ingredients used rather than their shape.

Since much of the enjoyment of your koi is seeing them feed at the surface, floating foods are recommended. Floating pellets also have the advantage in that you can determine if you are overfeeding, as with sinking pellets it is often difficult to assess whether all the food fed has been consumed. If food remains on the pond bottom too long it will decay, contributing to deterioration of the pond-water quality.

# Evaluating Commercial Diets

Although there are numerous commercial feed formulations available on the market, not all are suitable for koi. From a scientific standpoint, diets range from those that are hazardous for use in feeding fish to high-quality formulations that conform to scientific standards.

The quality of commercial foods varies. You should be careful to purchase only those that are formulated specifically for feeding koi. There are many available and they come in various sizes for feeding small or large fish.

Various criteria are employed in the evaluation of commercial formulas. As discussed above, certain percentages of protein, fat, fiber, minerals, and vitamins must be present to constitute a quality diet.

as supplements for feeding koi. Many of these are excellent sources of pigment, especially shrimp.

**Prepared foods:** Very popular for feeding koi, they are available as sinking or floating pellets, as well as flakes. There are numerous formulations such as maintenance pellets, color diets, vegetable diets, wheat germ, and others. While the nutritional claims of many formulations are accurate, you should scrutinize the label ingredients carefully.

Pelleted foods are sold in a variety of shapes and sizes, either floating or sinking. Koi show little preference as to the shape of the food and will consume either stick or pellet formulations. There is no scientific evidence to sug-

# Feeding for Good Color

The Japanese term *ironage* (ee-ro-na-gay) indicates the process of maximizing the color of koi. The development of good color is based on two major factors: the genetic color potential of the fish and the type of diet given. The appearance of the color can be affected by water quality as well. If the water temperature is higher than recommended for koi, the colors can appear to have a "bleached out" appearance. Simply reducing the water temperature can restore a more natural appearance to the fish.

Not all koi have the genetic potential to develop maximum color brilliance, as this is more directly related to the type and concentration of skin pigments. Often young fish have good pigmentation, but as they mature their pigmentation changes, sometimes improving and other times becoming worse. This underlines the importance of carefully selecting quality koi from reputable suppliers.

Naturally occurring pigments are found in various ingredients used for formulating prepared diets for koi. For example, examine the list of ingredients on the label of a container of koi food pellets. Look for items such as shrimp meal, plankton, marigold petals, chlorella, and spirulina. Each of these is a source of pigments that can enhance the color of koi.

**Spirulina:** This, in particular, has become a popular ingredient in foods due to its superior ability to enhance koi color. It is a freshwater blue-green algae of worldwide distribution. It is renowned for its high protein and vitamin content, and also possesses a high concentration of pigments, especially *beta-carotene*. As many koi breeders are aware, the inclusion of spirulina in the diet will particularly enhance red, orange, and yellow colors in koi.

**Carotenoids:** Freeze-dried foods, especially plankton, daphnia, and brine shrimp, contain high concentrations of compounds called *carotenoids*, a major pigment in the skin of koi.

# Feeding Procedures

## When to Feed

Fish should be fed several times a day, preferably in early morning, midafternoon, and late afternoon. Although it is popular to feed fish only during the morning and afternoon, recent study of koi digestion has indicated that they should be fed more frequently and in smaller amounts. When fed in this manner they are able to utilize carbohydrates more efficiently.

Young fish should be fed more often than adult fish.

## Amount to Feed

The amount of food given on a daily basis depends on numerous factors, including age, water temperature, and food quality. For good health and growth, they should receive 1 to 4 percent of their body weight per feeding. The upper figure is applicable to young growing koi. In practice, it is unnecessary to attempt such calculations; rather, it is recommended to feed small amounts and to observe the koi carefully over time. Adjust the amount of food according to growth rate and overall appearance.

The determination of the actual amount to be given is extremely difficult, and depends on various factors including the water temperature, number of koi, and their age. Care must also be exercised to prevent overfeeding, as koi can be gluttonous. Any excess food must be

═══ **TIP** ═══

### Food Storage

Store all foods, especially color foods, in cool areas, since the majority of color pigments are easily destroyed by heat.

✔ Prepared foods containing high amounts of pigments should be stabilized with some type of antioxidant.

✔ *Ethoxyquin* is a common antioxidant added to fish diets, and is known to effectively prevent the destruction of pigments during storage.

removed from the pond if it is not consumed within 20 minutes. By that time, uneaten food has lost many important nutrients, especially vitamins, to leaching.

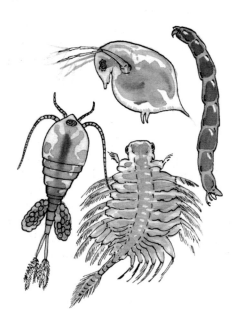

Make sure all of the fish are receiving some food by scattering it in slightly different, but adjacent areas. This method is recommended to prevent larger fish from consuming larger quantities of food and preventing slower, smaller fish from eating.

### Water Temperature

Water temperature must also be considered when feeding. Koi consume more food in warmer water than in cooler. The amount of food should therefore be adjusted according to seasonal water temperatures.

# Feeding in Different Seasons

### Fall and Winter

The fall and winter seasons will have a noticeable effect on the behavior and feeding habits of your fish. The amount of food required to feed your koi will need to be reduced as the water temperature decreases during the fall and winter. In regions with cold winter temperatures, fish will stop eating completely. In temperate areas, they will simply reduce the amount and frequency of their food intake. The reduced feeding activity is the direct result of the lowered metabolism of the fish. Lowered temperatures mean slower digestion times in the intestinal tract because of the reduced activity of certain digestive enzymes.

*Various live foods are suitable for feeding juvenile koi, including (clockwise from the top) daphnia, blood worms, brine shrimp, and cyclops.*

Koi should be fed well-balanced, quality diets during the growing season to prepare them for the winter. Many hobbyists switch from maintenance diets to wheat germ-formulated diets. Although this has been popular in practice, there is insufficient scientific evidence to suggest that wheat germ makes any significant difference for overwintering.

As water temperatures decline, decrease the amount of food you feed to your koi. Do not abruptly cease feeding, but carefully observe the fish's behavior and continue to feed until they stop showing interest. You will see reduced feeding activity when the temperature dips below 50°F (10°C). Do not continue feeding at that point.

## Spring and Summer

As the winter season ends and spring arrives, profound changes occur in the fish's physiology. Caution should be used in offering too much food at the beginning of the growing season. Bear in mind that the koi's digestive system, including secretion of enzymes, has been virtually shut down throughout the winter, especially in those fish overwintered in colder regions.

The best approach is to start feeding small amounts once the water temperature has reached 60°F (15.5°C). Begin feeding once a day, then slowly increase the amount of food as the water warms. Avoid giving too much food to your koi. Rely on careful observations of the koi's behavior. It is better to underfeed than to overfeed.

It should be pointed out that overfeeding of prepared dry foods in colder water in the spring can sometimes induce intestinal block-

---

**TIP**

**Prompting Fat Storage**

The key point is to reduce the protein in the diet and to increase carbohydrates and fat slightly to promote fat storage for utilization during cold weather. If the fish are fed a balanced, high-quality diet throughout the growing season, they will naturally begin to accumulate fat stores in preparation for the winter season.

---

age. Affected koi will exhibit several signs, most of which are quite obvious:

✔ First, the fish will appear to have difficulty swimming. This is most often related to a buoyancy problem.

✔ Second, the fish will develop abdominal distention, due to the accumulation of fluids in the abdominal cavity.

✔ It is important to note, however, that these signs are similar to those caused by bacterial infections and other disease agents; therefore, it is easy to misdiagnose the problem.

# Food Storage

Foods must be properly stored away from heat and moisture to preserve their quality. Leaving bags of flakes or pellets open to the air causes deterioration. Toxic substances can be produced by the growth of microbial contaminants, fat oxidation, and growth of molds and other organisms. Infestation by insects, including ants and weevils, can easily occur.

# QUARANTINE

*Quarantining new koi prior to introduction to your pond can prevent the inadvertent introduction of various diseases. Although new fish may appear healthy, there is always a possibility that they could transmit a disease agent.*

The practice of quarantining new fish prior to introduction to your pond is an important procedure than can prevent the inadvertent introduction of various infectious diseases. Even though newly purchased fish will appear to be in good health, they may be carriers of disease agents, including parasites, bacteria, and viruses.

## Fish That Should Be Quarantined

It is important not to overstock the pond during the first four to six weeks, as it takes that much time to condition the biological filter. It is also necessary to perform the water tests for ammonia, nitrite, nitrate, and pH every few days for the first several weeks to ensure that the values do not reach toxic levels. The first group of fish should be quarantined, if at

*Newly acquired koi must be placed in quarantine and examined carefully. They should be checked for any lesions or parasites.*

all possible, before their introduction to the pond. There is a reason why this is especially important: If the new fish are carrying a disease, it could necessitate treatment of the pond system. As previously noted, the necessary chemicals and antibiotics could affect the biological filter bacteria and damage plants.

Any new koi that you purchase thereafter will also need to be quarantined. Even if the fish you purchase have gone through a quarantine period, you should still place them in your own quarantine tank as a safety measure.

## The Quarantine Tank

You must have the quarantine tank ready and conditioned prior to the addition of any fish. The container must be used exclusively for quarantine and treatment purposes. Various containers are suitable for quarantine, including large aquariums and fiberglass holding tanks. For quarantining smaller juvenile fish, a tank of 50 to 125 gallons (189–473 L) should be ample. For quarantining larger koi,

10 inches (25 cm) or more, the quarantine tank should be at least 150 to 250 gallons (568–946 L).

**Important:** Never crowd too many fish in the quarantine tank as this will additionally stress the fish.

## Locating and Equipping the Quarantine Tank

The isolation tank should be located in an area away from the main pond and out of direct sunlight. It should be equipped with a biological filter and, in some cases, a heater. Providing aeration is important to ensure good water circulation, proper gas exchange, and high dissolved oxygen levels.

All quarantine tanks should be covered to prevent the koi from jumping out.

# Receiving New Koi

With newly acquired koi, check the pH and water temperature of the quarantine tank, and verify that the filter is functioning properly.

*Quarantine containers must be tightly covered with a screened top to prevent fish from jumping out of the tank.*

✔ Place the box with the koi in a shaded area. It is important to open the lid of the styrofoam box slowly and in dim light so as not to stress the fish any further. If the box is opened in sunlight the fish will become frightened and may begin to jump.

✔ Before adding the fish to the quarantine tank make sure the water temperature in the tank is close to the temperature of the water in the shipping bag.

✔ Place the container in the quarantine tank and allow the two water temperatures to equilibrate. Normally, if the koi are being moved from cooler water to slightly warmer water, there is less chance of thermal shock.

✔ When everything is ready, place the shipping bag into the tank water, open it, and gently tip the fish into the water. Carefully guide them from the bag into the tank, at the same time minimizing the amount of water spilling over into the tank from the shipping bag. In some cases, if the koi are small enough you can reach into the bag and lift the koi out. The use of a net is not recommended, since this can injure their skin.

✔ Cover the tank securely with a screen top to prevent the fish from jumping out. Start the quarantine period procedure as previously outlined.

After the fish have been released and have acclimated for several hours, try to examine them. Because any physical injury can invite infection by bacteria or fungi, it may be necessary to institute some type of treatment immediately.

In examining the koi, ask yourself a series of questions:

✔ Are there any skin lesions, raised scales, open wounds, or frayed fins?
✔ Is labored respiration evident?
✔ Is there frequent or occasional scratching?
✔ Are any white spots present on the body?
✔ Are the eyes protruding or turbid?
✔ Is there a general white or gray cloudiness to the skin?
✔ Are there any tumorlike growths?

These signs are useful in making a diagnosis. For example, frequent scratching and heavy respiration could indicate external parasites such as flukes. Protruding eyes could indicate a systemic bacterial infection.

Koi should be permitted to acclimate to the quarantine conditions for 24 to 48 hours before administration of any medications. The exception is the use of antibiotics, which will be necessary if lesions are noticed on the body. Fish can be fed sparingly during the initial 48-hour period if they show interest.

# Treating the Fish

## Quarantine Period

A quarantine period of 21 to 30 days is recommended for all fish. Although 21 days is the minimum, 30 days should be allowed as a safety measure if at all possible. Fish that have developed severe infestations from protozoan parasites such as *ich* should be quarantined for longer periods.

## Water-Quality Testing and Monitoring

You will need to make regular water tests during the quarantine period to ensure opti-

mum water quality. You should perform water tests including pH, ammonia, nitrite, and nitrate. If the parameters are abnormal, such as high ammonia, make a partial water change and then retest the water. Use a good-quality water conditioner during water changes to remove any chlorine or chloramine.

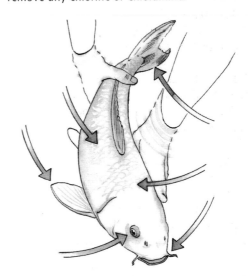

*Carefully examine fish for signs of disease. Look for any lesions on the tail, parasites on the body surface, ragged fins, tumors on the head, cloudy eyes, or abrasions on the snout.*

*Quarantine facilities should always be equipped with their own filtration systems and be covered with a mesh netting to prevent the fish from jumping out of the container.*

*You should make frequent observations of your koi during the quarantine period, looking for any abnormalities, such as frayed fins or abrasions on the skin.*

Treat water again with parasiticides and make partial water changes as required.

**Note:** Water changes are an important part of the quarantine period. They serve to reduce built-up organics, dilute residues from chemicals used to treat the fish, and reduce the number of parasites in the tank.

## Observing Your Fish

The fish must be examined several times each day to assess their progress. Fish treated for various diseases should begin showing improvement within three to five days.

Some fish's condition may improve faster than others in the group. However, even if one or two fish appear to have recovered, do not transfer them to the pond. More often than not, they are still carrying the disease agent. If you have any reason to believe the fish are still ill, hold them in quarantine for an additional seven to ten days.

## Feeding Your Fish During Quarantine

Be careful to feed your fish only lightly during the quarantine period. Often they will not eat for several days after transfer to the tank. However, you need not be alarmed at this; it is a natural response.

If you are treating your fish for a bacterial infection and using medicated food, it is important to feed exactly the amount required each day. It is also preferable to feed at approximately the same time.

## Transfer to the Pond

After the quarantine period has elapsed and any necessary treatments have been administered, the koi can be safely transferred to the pond. A minimum period of 21 to 30 days should elapse before this is done. You should reexamine the koi carefully prior to transferring them. If you have reason to believe that they are still parasitized or infected, conduct several more treatments and maintain them in quarantine for an additional seven to ten days.

# Basic Treatments

Various chemicals are used to eradicate disease agents. Improperly used, these chemicals can be toxic to fish. Some have very narrow safety margins, so care must be exercised.

It is desirable, whenever possible, to positively identify the disease agent before selecting a chemical treatment. Although this can seem complicated at first, some of the most common disease problems can be easily recognized (see page 82).

**Common table salt (noniodized only):** This is useful as a treatment for koi and is relatively safe. Its addition to water can perform two functions: easing osmoregulation and reducing stress. Salt added to water makes the ambient environment somewhat similar to the fish's body fluids, reducing the energy need. For this purpose, approximately 4 teaspoons per 10 gallons (20 g per 36.4 L) of water will produce a 0.05 percent solution.

Salt can also be used to treat parasites, but must be applied at much stronger dosages.

Special aquarium and pond salts are available from garden and pond centers and pet stores that give complete information on use for eradication of parasitic diseases.

**Formalin/malachite green medications:** These are commonly sold under various trade-names, including Ridlck. These medications are excellent for the control of various protozoans that attack koi. The mixture is so effective that many parasites are eradicated with a single treatment.

**Methylene blue:** A standard chemical used for the eradication of parasites and fungus, methylene blue has been widely used for the control of external parasites, and is relatively nontoxic compared to formalin and malachite green. Its chief disadvantage is that it stains porous materials.

**Organophosphates:** These are excellent for use during quarantine to control external parasites, such as fish lice, copepods, and trematodes. The active ingredient is also present in various medications sold for eradication of internal parasites, such as anchorworms or flukes.

Various other medications are available for treating diseases. You should consult with your local pet retailer, garden and pond center, or koi breeder for additional information.

## Using Chemicals Safely

There are some fundamental guidelines to using any type of chemical to treat koi. Not following these can interfere with the eradication of the disease, as well as posing possible toxicity hazards to the koi.

Any remedy must be used as directed on the label, and for the appropriate time period. Environmental conditions, including pH, hardness, temperature, and other parameters should be considered, as they may have an effect on the efficacy of the chemical. For example, organophosphates are administered at lower dosages when added to water with an acid pH, as they remain active for longer periods under those conditions. In alkaline water, however, they are destroyed within 24 to 48 hours, so that under those conditions a greater amount must be administered more frequently.

# Disinfecting Equipment

One of the most important ways to prevent the transfer of diseases from quarantine tanks to your pond is to make sure anything that comes into contact with the quarantine aquarium is disinfected after use. Many disease agents affecting koi, including bacteria, protozoa, and viruses, are easily transmitted. Just rinsing equipment in water is insufficient to destroy these agents. Nor is simple air-drying of nets or buckets considered a method of disinfection. Many viruses and parasites, especially those that produce spores, can withstand air-drying. Disinfectants must be used to prevent disease transmission from one pond to another.

## Disinfectants

Various disinfectants are available commercially for treating nets and related pond equipment. The majority are either chlorine or surfactant-active compounds. The latter are popular, and include the benzalkonium chloride class of compounds. These disinfectants are safe, generally odorless, and do not stain.

---

## TIP

### Avoiding Disease Transmission

It is not recommended that plastic bags be reused to transmit fish to other ponds or shows or to transport items to other koi ponds—various disease agents, especially viruses, could be transmitted. If you must reuse a bag, it needs to be disinfected completely with approved disinfectants such as benzalkonium chloride.

---

**Surfactant-type disinfectants:** These are widely used in hospitals, zoos, and food-production facilities. They have a wide spectrum of activity, and are effective against various disease-causing organisms. Concentrated solutions must be diluted prior to use. If the solution is used for net disinfection, it is important to rinse the net thoroughly with fresh water after disinfection and before use, as the disinfectant can be toxic. As with any chemical, the instructions provided on the label must be strictly followed to minimize any possible problems.

**Chlorine-based products:** These products also give excellent results, and are routinely used for disinfecting equipment and nets. When added to water, these compounds are extremely effective in destroying common disease agents. Some disadvantages are their sharp odor and their propensity to corrode equipment, such as nets, with repeated usage. They are, however, readily available, inexpensive, and easily neutralized using common water dechlorinators containing sodium thiosulfate.

# COMMON KOI DISEASES AND TREATMENTS

*Koi are susceptible to a wide number of disease agents. Although they are hardy fish, it is possible that they could be affected, especially if they come in contact with newly acquired nonquarantined fish.*

Maintaining water quality is critical for good fish health. Deterioration of the aquatic environment leads to stress, decreased resistance, and the emergence of disease.

## Stress and Fish Health

Research by fisheries scientists has shown that in natural populations there is a complex relationship between fish and the disease organisms that infect them. This accounts for the fact that fish in the wild can be found to harbor potential disease agents without exhibiting clinical signs of the disease. Thus, often newly purchased koi may appear to be in excellent health, but develop diseases after transport to your pond. Though they had previ-

*Koi are hardy fish, but can develop diseases if subjected to poor water quality, other nonquarantined fish, or poor nutrition.*

ously been asymptomatic, the stress of the move depressed their immune responses, allowing the growth of the pathogenic organism.

Fish are well protected with both nonspecific and specific (immune system) defenses. As long as the fish is in good health, these protective mechanisms are fully capable of preventing development of the disease.

Stress is the overall physiological response of an organism to perceived danger. For example, when you net a fish or reach into its pond, you induce a stress response.

If the degree and duration of the stress is too great, damage, or even death, can occur. Stress has a profound effect on the health of the fish, with the immune system being especially vulnerable.

Diseases develop when there is an imbalance between the pathogen and the host, resulting from a decrease in immunity. This imbalance can be initiated by unfavorable conditions such

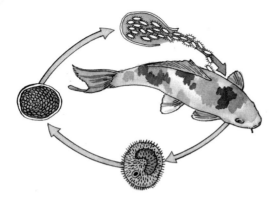

*The common protozoan, Ichthyophthirius multifiliis develops as small white spots on the koi's body. Upon maturation, the parasite drops off the fish to the pond bottom where it encysts and releases small tomites that can reinfect the koi.*

medicine who can examine your koi and prescribe medications that are not commercially available over-the-counter.

as high concentrations of ammonia or carbon dioxide, low dissolved oxygen, excessive handling, crowding, and poor nutrition.

# Identifying Diseases

First, perform a series of standard water tests to ensure that the problem is not directly related to poor water quality.

Many diseases are easy to diagnose by observing typical behavioral changes or body lesions. However, many of the lesions caused by parasites are similar in their appearance. Therefore, recognition of the parasite is important in order to confirm the diagnosis.

Once the disease is identified, select an appropriate course of treatment. You may need to treat with an antimicrobial agent, or one designed to eradicate certain parasites. Some medications are *broad spectrum* and are effective against a wide range of pathogenic organisms; others are effective against only one or a few.

It is important to note that in some instances, a disease problem can be so difficult to diagnose and treat that you should obtain professional assistance. There are a number of veterinarians who trained in aquatic animal

# Basic Medications and Techniques

Many medications are available commercially for the treatment of koi diseases. You should rely on your professional pet store owner, koi breeder, or professional pond and garden center for the proper selection and use of medications.

**Antimicrobials:** These include a variety of drugs designed to control and eradicate microorganisms such as bacteria, fungi, and viruses.

**Parasiticides:** These are medications indicated for the treatment of parasitic disease agents such as protozoans (*Chilodonella, Ichthyobodo,* etc.), trematodes (flukes), tapeworms, leeches, and copepods. Various commercially produced parasiticides are available for treating fish in ponds and quarantine tanks.

**Combined formulations:** Some brands of fish medications combine both parasiticides and antimicrobials into proprietary formulations. In developing these combinations, manufacturers mix different compatible medications to control a wide spectrum of disease agents.

## Administration Techniques

Disease outbreaks can be treated using various methods, including addition to the water, administration in the food, or injection. The latter technique is excellent for treating fish, but requires training and should be used with caution.

**Dipping:** This is characterized by an exposure period ranging from several seconds to several minutes. The fish are removed from the pond, placed in a basin of water to which the medication has been added, then removed after the predetermined treatment period. The dip method is repeated several times, depending on the disease and the type of drug. The disadvantage of this method is that it is stressful, since the fish must be handled as well as exposed to higher drug concentrations.

**Extended baths:** Baths are a safer and more commonly used method. The fish are exposed to a more dilute solution of the medication for a longer period, generally lasting several hours or more depending on the type of drug, its toxicity, and the disease being treated.

**Adding medications to the food:** This method is a useful method of administration, often used to eradicate systemic bacterial infections and internal parasites. To eradicate tapeworms, for example, a drug must be administered in the food. Several commercial food preparations are sold that incorporate antibacterials or parasiticides.

# Treatment Guidelines

The following guidelines should be followed whenever you are treating koi in ponds or in quarantine facilities. It is important to understand that treating fish is a serious matter, and must be approached with caution. Carelessness could result in possible mortalities.

## Identify the Disease Prior to Treatment

Although as a koi pond owner you are not likely to become an expert in disease diagnosis, you should be able to recognize several of the most common koi disease problems. Identifying the disease prior to treatment allows the selection of a more appropriate treatment regime.

## Adding Chemicals to Ponds

It is preferable to treat diseased fish in separate quarantine facilities; the addition of chemicals to ponds should be avoided, although this is not always possible. Chemicals added to the pond can cause many problems, including damage to plants and biological filters, and necessitate the need for large-volume water changes between treatments.

Prior to using any chemical in the pond or quarantine tank, you should be aware of possible effects on the filter bacteria. Some chemicals will cause a suppression or complete cessation of the filter-bed activity, with the subsequent increase in the level of toxic ammonia. Two drugs known to adversely affect the biological filter bacteria are methylene blue and erythromycin. You should follow instructions carefully on the use of these and other drugs that you purchase for pond use.

## Observe the Behavior of the Fish During Treatment

Although it is intended to cure a disease, the addition of any chemical to water is nonetheless stressful to fish. The toxicity of drugs varies according to the type and strength of the medication. It is important to be cautious whenever using a chemical for the first time in a pond or treatment facility. A general rule is to test medications with a small group of fish prior to administration to a larger group. It is best to perform the treatment earlier in the day, so that you can observe their behavior. If they appear unduly stressed, make an immediate water change.

## Continue Water Testing During Treatment

Routine tests such as pH, ammonia, dissolved oxygen, etc., should be made throughout the duration of the treatment. A decline of water quality only worsens existing infections by further lowering the koi's resistance. Such conditions work against a rapid recovery of the fish under treatment.

## Make Water Changes

In addition to water tests, a regular series of water changes should be made throughout the treatment. Generally, a partial water change is required every 24 to 36 hours, after which the medicine is again administered.

There are various reasons why water changes are necessary during treatment of koi. Most importantly, water changes dilute concentrations of various toxic chemicals, including ammonia, organics, and degradation products resulting from the decomposition of the chemicals used during treatment. Reducing organics is especially important, since they bind up many chemicals such as malachite green, rendering the chemical useless for parasite control. Water changes also dilute the concentration of parasites or bacteria, helping to accelerate recovery of the koi.

## Discontinue Chemical Filtration During Treatments

Activated carbon is effective in removing chemicals from the water, including such medications as malachite green, formalin, and antibiotics. It is essential to discontinue use of any activated carbon in your mechanical filters during fish treatments. However, the filters themselves should remain in full operation. Upon completion of the treatment, and after a water change, new chemically active media can be restored to the filter.

# Infectious Diseases

Infectious diseases are caused by a number of different types of organisms, among which the most important are parasites, including protozoans, various kinds of worms, and crustaceans, bacteria, fungi, and viruses.

## Protozoa

The protozoans are the most common disease agents affecting koi. These are one-celled, microscopic organisms that can reproduce rapidly in ponds.

Some parasites cannot survive outside of the host. These are called *obligate* parasites. If they can survive without their preferred hosts they are referred to as *opportunistic*.

Some diseases caused by protozoa are

**White spot disease:** This disease is caused by a ciliated organism called *Ichthyophthirius multifiliis*, nicknamed "ich" (pronounced "ik"). It attacks the skin and gills. The disease is serious, and must be treated rapidly to prevent mortalities.

Infected fish are listless, have clamped fins, (the fins have collapsed onto the body), lose their normal color, and are covered with small white spots on their body and fins. Affected koi often congregate near areas of water turbulence. They can also be observed to scratch themselves frequently on objects in the pond.

The life cycle of the parasite includes both attached and free-swimming forms. The control of ich focuses on the eradication of the free-swimming form.

The attached parasites, which can attain a size of 1 mm, drop off the fish when mature and sink to the bottom of the pond, where they encyst. Division occurs within the cyst, and a number of free-swimming individuals develop. The cyst eventually ruptures, releasing the parasites into the water, where they seek a fish to infect. The time required to complete the life cycle is temperature-dependent: The higher the temperature, the faster the cycle. For example, in water of 70 to 79°F (21–26°C), the life cycle is completed in less than a week, while in water at 50°F (10°C), the life cycle is extended to over a week.

Various commercial medications are effective for controlling ich. The active ingredients in these formulations are most often formalin, malachite green, salt, and potassium permanganate.

**Trichodinids:** *Trichodina* and related species such as *Trichodonella* are troublesome ciliated protozoa that commonly parasitize koi. They are capable of causing damage to the skin and gills, leading to secondary bacterial infections.

Affected fish frequently scratch themselves on the sides or bottom of the pond, have clamped fins, lose their normal coloration, and have difficult respiration. The skin develops small reddened ulcerations that gradually enlarge.

Most of the medications used for the treatment of ich are also suitable for eradication of trichodina. The parasites are sensitive to malachite green or formalin.

Because trichodinids multiply by simple cell division with no free-swimming form, usually only one or two treatments are required.

**Chilodonella** (*Chilodeonella cyprini*): This is a ciliated protozoan commonly affecting koi and goldfish. It is an obligate parasite that inhabits the skin and gills. When examined microscopically, it appears heart-shaped or oval. Infected fish develop a noticeable bluish white opaqueness of the skin, with excess mucus secretion. They will tend to scrape themselves on the pond bottom. Increased lethargy and an increased respiratory rate is often observed. Mortality is rapid, especially among juvenile fish. Treatments using malachite green, formalin, or salt dips are required for eradication of the parasite.

**Epistylis:** A ciliate known to attach to koi, the protozoan is not considered an obligate parasite, but will multiply under certain conditions, forming large, stalked colonies. Attachment to the host invites secondary infection by bacteria.

Koi affected by *Epistylis* develop white tuft-like areas, resembling fungus. As they grow, the areas become ulcerated, with a reddish ring surrounding the white area.

The presence of *Epistylis* is associated with poor water quality and high water temperatures.

**Chilodonella** *primarily affects the gills, causing extensive tissue damage and predisposing the fish to secondary bacterial infection.*

*Common parasitic worms (left to right): leech, monogenetic fluke, nematode.*

High levels of organic material in the pond water favor its development. It is easily controlled by the use of formalin-based medications.

**Ichthyobodo necatrix:** Formerly known as *Costia*, it is a small, flagellated protozoan. It is a troublesome parasite, attacking fish that have been previously stressed. The Japanese refer to this disease as *dorokaburi*, or "slime disease."

Affected fish develop a whitish film on their skin, are listless, and hold their fins close to their body. Conspicuous red lesions can also be present, and the fish will repeatedly scratch themselves on the pond bottom. Rapid, labored respiration is not uncommon.

Like other protozoa, *Ichthyobodo* is sensitive to medications containing malachite green, salt, or formalin.

**Sporozoans:** These are a group of troublesome parasites whose life cycle involves the production of large numbers of tough spores that can survive for long periods without a host. Although they are not as commonly encountered as other protozoa, it is important to be able to recognize the signs of infection. They form white nodules on the fins, skin, and gills, and produce light-colored lesions in the muscles.

No safe and effective treatments are available for sporozoan infestations. Affected fish must be removed from the pond to prevent possible transmission of the disease.

**Coccidians:** Coccidians are another group of protozoa capable of causing severe losses. The most frequently seen coccidial disease is known as nodular coccidiosis, caused by the organism *Eimeria cyprini*. Young koi are the most likely victims, sustaining damage to the intestinal lining. Affected fish can show a loss of color, have sunken eyes, and become thin. A yellowish color in the feces is characteristic of the disease. Various medications have been tried, but the disease is still considered untreatable. Affected fish must be removed from the pond to prevent transmission to other koi.

## Platyhelminths

The platyhelminths include various parasitic worms such as flukes and tapeworms. Many have complex life cycles requiring more than one host.

**Trematodes, or flukes:** These are a class of parasites divided according to their life cycle into two major groups: the *monogenes* and the *digenes*. Monogenetic trematodes are external parasites of the skin and gills that require only one host to complete their life cycle. The digenetic group is made up of internal parasites. They have a complex life cycle requiring more than one host.

*Monogenetic trematodes:* The pond owner should be primarily concerned with the monogenetic flukes, as they are common parasites of koi and other fish and can cause serious mortality increases.

*Gyrodactylus* and *Dactylogyrus:* These are two monogenetic genera that commonly infest koi.

The flukes attach to fish by means of a special attachment organ, called a *haptor*, that is equipped with hooks.

Affected fish show variable behavioral changes, depending on the severity of the infection. The

*Common protozoan parasites of koi (clockwise from the top left):* **Trichodina, Chilodonella,** *and* **Ichthyophthirius.**

most common clinical signs are increased rate of respiration, dull coloration, and excessive scratching on the pond bottom or on various objects. Serious infections involving the gills result in hemorrhaging, skin damage, and secondary bacterial infection.

Monogenetic trematodes are easily eradicated with commercial medications containing formalin. Products containing organophosphates, mebendazole, or praoziquantel are also useful for control of monogenetic flukes.

*Digenetic trematodes:* They have a complex life cycle, with a number of larval forms and several hosts. The first form, known as a *miracidium*, parasitizes snails. Here it develops into a cercariae. This form parasitizes a second host, either forming a *metacercariae* or maturing directly into the adult parasite. *Metacercariae* appear as nodules on various parts of the body, including eyes, gills, muscles, and skin. Eventually they transform into adults, which migrate to the intestinal tract.

Affected fish become listless, and a pattern of slow mortalities can develop. If the parasite is present in the gills, these will be pale, with swellings or cysts. Nodules can be present on the skin as well as on internal organs.

Generally, digenetic trematodes are not considered to be serious parasites of koi. Keeping snails out of the koi pond is a simple but effective way to prevent the development of the disease. Once the parasites have infested the fish, the disease is basically untreatable.

**Cestodes, or tapeworms:** Cestodes are flattened worms whose body is composed of a head and a number of segments called *proglottids*. The head bears an organ called a *scolex*, with which the worm attaches to the inner wall of the intestine. Tapeworms have complex life cycles requiring several hosts. Koi can be the intermediate or final host, depending on the species of tapeworm. The final hosts of some species are either birds or mammals. Larval forms can encyst in the peritoneal cavity or other areas of the fish's body.

Infestations are difficult to diagnose. Very few behavioral signs are observed. Severely infested fish can appear emaciated.

Most of the medications recommended for treatment must be added to the food in order to kill these internal parasites effectively. Recent research using the drug Praziquantel has indicated that it rapidly eradicates tapeworms from the gut. The drug is simply added to the water for use in a bath treatment.

## Nematodes

The nematodes are slender, unsegmented roundworms. In the larval form nematodes can be found in practically any organ or tissue of a fish. They are most common in the musculature, intestine, and liver.

Their life cycle involves intermediate hosts, the first usually being a copepod or insect. If a koi eats the intermediate hosts containing the larval nematodes, the worms will take up residence in the fish's gut. If the worms use the fish as an intermediate host, they will be found coiled in small nodules in the tissues or organs.

Affected fish exhibit poor appetite and loss of color. There are few drugs that are totally effective in eradicating nematodes. The best treatment is addition of the drug Panacur at a concentration of 0.25 percent.

## Annelids

The annelids are a group of worms containing both free-living and parasitic species. The best known of the free-living annelids is the common earthworm. The only type that is troublesome to koi are the leeches.

**Leeches:** Leeches are external parasites with a segmented body and anterior and posterior suckers. Most of the species affecting koi are visible with the naked eye.

The parasites feed on the host's blood, and when present in large enough numbers, especially in young fish, they can cause anemia. Leeches are more of an annoyance than a serious problem. They are, however, known to transmit bacterial diseases through the wounds they cut in the fish's skin.

Leeches can be eradicated by using a variety of drugs sold on the market.

**Note:** Always quarantine plants before placing them in the pond to prevent introduction of leeches or leech eggs.

## Crustaceans

Crustaceans are arthropods. Among the family are such well-known animals as shrimp and lobsters, but they also include numerous parasitic species.

**Argulus, or fish lice:** Argulus have flat bodies and can crawl freely over the fish's skin. In appearance they resemble flattened scales. Eggs are laid on submerged vegetation and other objects in the pond.

Affected fish show damaged, reddened skin surfaces and pinpoint hemorrhages. When examining the koi for the possible presence of parasites, look for small, scalelike, mottled, leaflike objects that move on the fish's body.

Fish lice can also invade the gills, so increased and labored respiration are signs associated with infestation. Many species are large enough to see with the naked eye or with the aid of a low-power magnifier.

Treatment is with a variety of commercial medications containing one or more of the following active ingredients: formalin, organophosphates, or potassium permanganate.

**Copepods:** These are small crustaceans, many of which are parasitic on koi. Specialized holdfast organs are present and the mouth parts are adapted to piercing the fish's body.

The anchorworm, *Lernaea cyprinacea*, is a common copepod parasite of koi. Although referred to as anchorworms, they are not really worms. Mature females produce eggs in strings, and these, trailing from the body of the fish, are diagnostic. Newly hatched larvae are immediately capable of infecting fish.

The presence of a few parasites is not serious, but untreated fish are likely to develop secondary bacterial infections.

These parasites can be controlled using commercially available products containing formalin, organophosphates, or diflubenzuron. The latter is sold under the trade name of Dimilin. The latter product is particularly effective and available in an easy-to-use liquid formulation. It is important to note that these products control the free-swimming juvenile stage of the parasite. Attached adult forms present on the fish are unaffected. If a few adult forms are present on the fish, they can be carefully removed with a pair of forceps. The area should then be swabbed with an external antiseptic such as a povidone iodine solution.

## Bacteria

Bacteria are unicellular, microscopic organisms commonly found in soil and water. They vary in shape and reproduce by simple division.

Bacterial infections are largely initiated by deteriorating water conditions, inducing stress that lowers normal resistance. Damaged skin is a common site for the establishment of bacteria. If left untreated, the infection progresses internally and can become systemic.

**Ulcer disease:** Also known as dropsy or abdominal distention, this disease is usually caused by *Aeromonas* or *Pseudomonas* bacteria. Affected fish show ulceration of the body, a swollen abdomen, protruding scales, and swollen eyes. Fish tend to be listless, stop eating, and lose their normal coloration.

Disease outbreaks are correlated with environmental factors. In koi, outbreaks usually occur in the spring, but the disease can also occur during the summer, especially if the fish are stressed by chronically low oxygen concentrations.

Ulcer disease can be treated by several methods using appropriate antibiotics. Tetracyline or oxytetracycline can be added at recommended dosages to the food and fed to the fish for 10 to 14 days or until no mortalities are observed in the pond. Medicated foods are also commercially available with added antibiotics. Another approach is the use of a tris-EDTA potentiated antibiotic Tricide-Neo. The medication is added to water and the affected koi dipped for a specific time period every other day. This powerful patented medication was developed by the University of Georgia, Athens, Georgia, and has

been found to be effective in controlling ulcer disease.

**Bacterial gill disease:** This disease can be caused by a number of species, the most common being *myxobacteria*. The condition has been linked to overcrowding, high levels of organics, and other related environmental conditions, and can cause extensive mortalities. Some studies have shown that in the earlier stages of development, progression can be reversed simply by reducing the population and flushing the pond with new water. The problem is uncommon in ponds that have low fish populations and good water quality. Outbreaks have also been correlated with abnormally high temperatures.

Affected fish appear lethargic and become abnormally pale, with excess mucus present on the skin. Respiratory distress is common, and infected individuals can be observed near the pond surface or in agitated areas. Large white areas of dead tissue are found in the gills. Secondary fungal infections are also observed. Large quantities of bacteria are seen in microscopic examination of skin scrapings.

Several approaches can be used in controlling bacterial gill disease. Antibacterials have been found useful.

**Mycobacteriosis:** A well-known disease, having been reported in koi as early as 1897, it is

*Two common crustacean parasites: Argulus, the fish louse (top), and Lernaea cyprinacea, the common anchorworm.*

caused by the organism *Mycobacteria*, which produces characteristic lesions, called granulomas, in the internal organs. The condition is difficult to diagnose, as the signs are not always specific. Mycobacteriosis is a chronic and progressive disease. Fish develop ulcerations, swollen eyes, and abdominal distention. Diagnosis is confirmed only from an internal examination of the fish, which is itself a lethal procedure.

There is no therapy for mycobacteriosis. Fish suspected of having the disease should be removed from the pond to prevent transmission to other fish.

## Fungal Infections

Fungal infections are frequently encountered in koi, usually appearing after transport or in association with other diseases, especially those involving parasites. Fungi are generally secondary invaders, typically developing on wounds.

**Saprolegniasis:** This is a fairly common condition, characterized by the presence of whitish threads on the skin and fins of koi. The fungus is recognized by its cottony-white appearance, and is easily seen with the naked eye. The large, grayish white lesions sometimes have a reddish perimeter. Algae can sometimes be seen associated with the lesions. This fungus is usually found on the skin, but also occurs on damaged gill tissue. Infection of the gills is extremely serious and must be treated immediately to prevent mortality.

During early stages of the disease, the fungus can be eradicated quickly, but it is more diffi-

cult to cure as it progressively invades the fish's body. Commercial medications containing malachite green are particularly effective, and methylene blue, salt, and formalin are also useful.

**Branchiomycosis:** Called *erakusaribyo* by the Japanese, this is a disease of the gills. Unlike *Saprolegnia*, this fungus is partial to intravascular tissue, and invades the gills directly. It is believed that infection is initiated by ingestion of fungal spores.

Affected fish show extreme respiratory distress and hemorrhages, and patches of dead gill tissue are seen. Fish can succumb to the disease within several days.

Currently there is no known treatment. It is important to isolate any suspected fish.

## Viral Infections

Viruses are extremely small infective agents that can multiply only within the living cells of the host. The best-known fish viruses infect salmon and trout, but several are known to attack koi.

Viral infections are best avoided by carefully quarantining fish suspected of carrying them. It is impossible to diagnose the majority of viral infections from physical examination, although a few produce characteristic lesions.

**Spring viremia of carp (SVCV):** This has often been described as dropsy or abdominal distention. The disease was once thought to be a complex condition, initiated by bacteria and followed by a viral invasion, but it is now known to be caused by a single agent, *Rhabdovirus carpio*.

Various signs are associated with the disease, among which are swollen eyes, hemorrhages of the skin and gills, inability to swim, and swollen abdomen. Affected fish also become darker in color and stay in areas of the pond where the water is agitated. Koi of any age group can be affected, but the disease is particularly serious in younger koi. The disease tends to be most prevalent in the early spring as water temperatures begin to increase. Extensive mortalities are common.

The disease is highly contagious. Viral particles are shed into the water via the feces, generally entering the fish through the gills. Fish that survive the infection can be carriers for life. Neither treatment nor control is known. However, treatment with appropriate antibiotics can help to resolve any secondary bacterial infections. Suspected fish must be removed from the pond.

The disease can easily be misdiagnosed as intestinal blockage caused by overfeeding.

**Koi herpes virus (KHV) disease:** A highly contagious disease of koi, it was first confirmed from an outbreak in 1999 from common carp in Israel. The virus is classified as a herpes virus and the first outbreak in the United States was documented in 2000. It is important to note that this virus is not transmissible to humans, as it can affect only koi, and is not transmissible to other pond fish such as goldfish.

Affected fish that come into contact with diseased fish can develop the disease within 14 days. Recent research indicates that the disease most often appears in water temperatures between 64 and 81°F (18–27°C). The virus produces gill lesions that upon gross appearance

seem to mottle with patches of white. The appearance is somewhat similar to other gill bacterial infections.

Affected fish, water, and sediments transmit the disease. Currently, there is no known treatment for it. Suspected fish require the intervention by a veterinarian to confirm the disease.

The disease can be minimized by quarantining all new fish for 30 days prior to introduction to a pond, not displaying fish at koi shows in the same pools with other fish, and disinfecting all equipment used when transferring fish from one pond or tank to another.

**Carp pox:** This disease has been known for more than 400 years, yet it is not often recognized as a viral disease by koi pond owners. It is caused by a virus belonging to the *herpes* group, is considered chronic and not life-threatening, and often develops during the early spring season.

Affected fish develop small, white, opaque, plaquelike raised areas on various parts of the body. These gradually enlarge. The lesions are smooth, and can be tinged pink due to a heavy development of capillaries within the tissue.

There is no treatment, but the lesions often disappear as water temperatures increase.

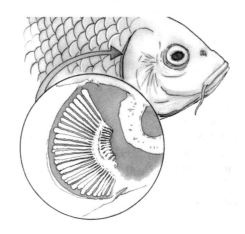

*Gill disease can be caused by numerous types of bacteria. Infection results in the destruction and erosion of the delicate filaments. Deteriorating water quality has been linked to the development of this disease.*

# INFORMATION

## Miscellaneous Organizations and Agencies

**Associated Koi Clubs of America**
P.O. Box 1
Midway City, CA 92655
*www.akca.org*

**Midwest Pond and Koi Society**
P.O. Box 1251
North Riverside, IL 60546
*www.mpks.org*

**Canada Koi Club of BC**
131-720 6th Street
New Westminster, B.C. V3L3C5
*www.canadakoiclub.ca*

## Useful Web Sites

**Van Ness Water Gardens**
*www.vnwg.com*

**Lilypons Water Gardens**
*www.lilypons.com*

**Laguna Koi Ponds**
*www.lagunakoi.com*

## Koi, Pond, and Related Magazines

*Koi USA*
P.O. Box 1
Midway City, CA 92655

*Butterfly koi have a beautiful silvery and gold metallic sheen due to special cells in their skin called iridocytes.*

*Koi Carp Magazine*
Freestyle Publications Ltd
Alexander House, Ling Road, Tower Park,
Poole, Dorset, England BH12 4 NZ

*Freshwater and Marine Aquarium Magazine*
P.O. Box 487
Sierra Madre, CA 91025

## Books

Swindells, P. *Waterfalls and Fountains.*
Hauppauge, New York: Barron's Educational
Series, Inc., 2002.
Swindells, P. *Pond Features and Decoration.*
Hauppauge, New York: Barron's Educational
Series, Inc., 2002.

*Koi swimming in a pond.*

### About the Author

George Blasiola (B.S., M.A.) is a specialist in fish biology. He was formerly associated with the Steinhardt Aquarium, California Academy of Sciences, San Francisco as an aquatic biologist. As chief consultant to the City of San Jose, Japanese Friendship Gardens, from 1975-1985, he helped redesign the extensive pond systems and set up a comprehensive fish health husbandry program for the city's Koi collection. Mr. Blasiola was the former Director of Research and Development for the Wardley Corporation, where his emphasis was the re-formulation and introduction of a new series of aquarium, marine, and fish foods. He is currently a consultant for Aqua-Sphere Research, his consulting company in California. He has published more than 100 articles on fish health, pond management, fish nutrition, fish biology, fish parisitology, and related topics in scientific journals and popular magazines. His research has focused on the identification and control of diseases of pond and marine fish, and the role of nutrition in the preventing of fish diseases.

Mr. Blasiola was the annual lecturer at the University of Georgia's Fish Health Workshop from 1982-1999 and is currently guest lecturer at the University of North Carolina's Fish Health Seminar. He has lectured at various professional meetings, including the American Fishes Society; the International Association of Aquatic Animal Medicine; the University of California, Davis; Hayward State University's Musee Oceanographique, Monaco; the Australian Rainbow Fish Association, Sydney; Associated Koi Clubs of America Annual Meeting; Texas A & M University (Aqua Med); Oregon State University; and the DC Association of Veterinary Medicine.

He is contributing editor to *Freshwater and Marine Aquarium Magazine* and *Pet Age*, a review board member for the *Journal of Aquariculture and Aquatic Sciences*, and the author of Barron's *New Marine Aquarium Handbook.*

## Acknowledgments

Writing a book and making subsequent revisions to new editions does not happen in a vacuum. There are many individuals who are part of the creative and production process. My ongoing appreciation is extended to Tom Graham and Joyce Conrad of *Koi USA* magazine for their assistance in koi identification and contribution of photos; Bob Spindola for supplementary koi photo identification; Carl Fridenstine for his generous help in arranging for me to take new pond photos for the 2nd edition; Dr. Robert Rofen and Verle Parker for the use of the Aquatic Research Library; Wyatt LeFever of Blue Ridge Fish Hatchery for use of the butterfly koi photo; Dr. John B. Gratzek for use of the koi pox photo; Dr. Gregory Lewbart for providing koi anatomy photos; Scott Massey for koi pond photos; Michele Earle-Bridges for the preparation of the original illustrations; and Dave Rodman of Barron's, who helped me get through the process of getting the 2nd edition ready.

## Photo Credits

Blue Ridge Fish Hatchery: 92; George Blasiola: 2–3, 4, 16, 20 (top and bottom), 21, 25 (top), 28, 29, 33 (top and middle), 36, 37, 40, 44, 45, 48, 53, 56, 60, 61, 64, 72, 76, 80, 85, and 93; *Koi USA*: 8 (all photos), 9 (all photos), 12 (all photos), 24 (top left and right), and 41; Scott Massey (Animal Kingdom): 24 (bottom), 25 (bottom), 32 (top and bottom), 33 (bottom), and 68; and Anthony Terceira: 5, 17, 49, 57, 65, 73, 77, and 81.

## Cover Photos

Inside back cover: Eric Crichton © Interpet Publishing; front cover: Geoff Rogers © Interpet Publishing; inside front cover and back cover: Anthony Terceira.

## Important Note

Before using any of the electrical equipment described in this book, be sure to read Avoiding Electrical Accidents (page 22).

## Dedication

This book is dedicated to my dear friend Sue Busch, pet-industry leader and benefactor, whose vision, leadership, and commitment to pet-care education have helped make the American pet industry stronger.

*All inquiries should be addressed to:*
Barron's Educational Series, Inc.
250 Wireless Boulevard
Hauppauge, NY 11788
**www.barronseduc.com**

Library of Congress Catalog Card No. 2004058052

International Standard Book No. 0-7641-2852-3

**Library of Congress Cataloging-in-Publication Data**
Blasiola, George C.
   Koi : everything about care, nutrition, diseases,
   pond design and maintenance, and popular
   aquatic plants; illustrations by Michele
   Earle-Bridges.—2nd ed.
     p. cm.
   ISBN 0-7641-2852-3 (alk. paper)
    1. Koi. I. Title.

SF458.K64B58  2005
639.3'7483—dc22          2004058052

Printed in China

9 8 7 6 5 4 3 2 1